$3 Low-Calorie Meals

Delicious, Low-Cost Dishes That Won't Add to Your Waistline

Ellen Brown

The Lyons Press
Guilford, Connecticut
An imprint of The Globe Pequot Press

This book is dedicated to Ed Claflin, my agent, whose support and encouragement are appreciated every day.

To buy books in quantity for corporate use
or incentives, call **(800) 962–0973**
or e-mail **premiums@GlobePequot.com.**

The Lyons Press is an imprint of The Globe Pequot Press.

Text design: Sheryl P. Kober

Library of Congress Cataloging-in-Publication Data is available on file.

ISBN 978-1-59921-821-2

Printed in the United States of America

10 9 8 7 6 5 4 3 2 1

Contents

Your wallet—not your waistline—will be fatter once you've started employing the money-saving tips in this chapter. It's all about advance planning, creating a good list, and using coupons efficiently.

Cooking is not an intuitive process; it's a collection of skills accumulated over the years. In this chapter you'll gain some new skills, all of which will reduce the calories in your meals.

There is a whole market niche in the supermarket for low-cal sauces and dressings, and most of them are filled with chemicals as well as being costly. You'll learn to make your own—for pennies—in this chapter.

These soups and appetizers are a way to begin a meal, or if a few of them are cooked and served together they become the meal. In addition to being low cost, they are also low cal!

Poultry meat is inherently low in calories; what creates a high-calorie dish is the skin and then how the birds are cooked. These are all recipes that are full of flavor that glorify the birds.

Pork, "the other white meat" as it's now advertised, is relatively low in calories as well as being lower in cost than most cuts of lean beef. In this chapter you'll learn myriad ways to prepare it, plus some low-cal versions of favorite beef dishes.

Chapter 7: Two If By Sea . . . Fish Entrees   **146**

There's no question that fish plays a central role in low-cal eating, and there are so many species to choose from that fish meals can be a part of your regular food budget.

Chapter 8: Vibrant and Vegetarian Entrees   **189**

What you'll learn about the recipes from this chapter is that low-cal vegetable dishes are hardly "bunny food!" These are satisfying, hearty entrees that will satisfy your soul as well as your stomach.

Chapter 9: (Almost) Guilt-Free Goodies   **219**

You *can* have your cake and eat it, too! And you can also have muffins, mousses, numerous fruit desserts, and some desserts made with luscious chocolate. Your sweet tooth will not feel deprived in any way eating these treats.

Preface

I understand and appreciate how hard it is to plan healthful meals for your family these days. That's where I can help you, and where this book comes in. *$3 Low-Calorie Meals,* as well as the other books in the *$3 Meals* series, is dedicated to helping you produce delicious meals that hide the fact that they're created on a budget, and in this case, keep it a secret that they're actually good for you. These recipes will prove to you that low-calorie can still mean high-flavor, and that the reduction of fat in foods will never be detected by your family and friends. You will keep everyone healthy and they will never even know it.

Here's the predicament in which we find ourselves. On one side there's the skyrocketing cost of food that challenges all of us shopping with a limited food budget. Even if the cost of gasoline drops back, prices at the supermarket will barely change, because the reasons for increasingly expensive food are global and not national.

For example, the conversion of wheat fields in Umbria to produce sunflowers for ethanol led to a great surge in the price of pasta—a place to which we always turn for the foundation for a low-cost meal—because there's a scarcity of durum wheat. And halfway around the world from this sun-drenched region of Italy, the long-awaited growth of a middle class in both India and China has given Western countries competition for the world's meat supply—and increased the cost of all meats we find in the supermarket.

Then on the other hand is the need to feed yourself and your family meals that are low in calories and high in nutrients for a healthy life. Obesity is an epidemic in America—for both adults *and* children.

All recent weight-loss research points to the truism that calories are what really make the difference. Plainly stated, with high-calorie meals you're sure to put on the pounds, and with low-calorie meals, losing weight or maintaining your best weight are going to be a whole lot easier. But calorie-counting is a pretty hateful process. With the recipes in this book, you don't have to bother. They're all low-calorie. Karen Konopelski, who holds a master's degree in nutrition, served as my consultant and analyzed all the recipes for their calories and other nutrients. So she and I have done the homework for you.

We all know that many foods that are low in cost are also low in nutrition, as well as being high in calories. Wearing one hat, you're supposed to be a bargain hunter—a fast and efficient forager—but then you're also asked to spend time reading food labels—and understanding what they mean. Shopping for food could take up a good part of your day! And it can't—because there's too much else to do in this time of scarce money.

But take heart! You don't need to read food labels and figure out nutritional values. I've done it for you, and each recipe in *$3 Low-Calorie Meals* has been analyzed by a dietitian so you know *exactly* how many calories you're consuming at every meal. And these are *real* foods, not those frozen low-calorie entrees from the supermarket that are loaded with chemicals and are more expensive per ounce than any recipe in this book.

There's a cornucopia of inexpensive vegetables in the produce aisle—and in the frozen food aisle—as well as other whole grain and complex carbohydrate foods that are what dietitians praise as being "nutrient dense." Those form the basis for these recipes. But a high percentage of vegetables and whole grains doesn't mean this is "bunny food."

Only a fraction of these recipes are vegetarian; most contain skinless poultry—yes, including the popular and lean boneless breasts—as well as fish and meats. You'll be eating beef and pork, just not a huge hunk. To control calories, these recipes reverse the proportions of meat to vegetables in the meat-centered American diet.

Not only isn't there a can of "cream of something soup" in any recipes—including the Low-Cal Tuna Noodle Casserole!—there aren't any processed foods at all. The more a food is processed, more expensive it becomes and the less healthy it is for you. Americans have been at the mercy of big business for too long. We don't need them in the kitchen. So get ready to peel and slice some carrots; it only takes a minute, and you can save the peels to make the stock you'll use for your soups.

But don't picture yourself spending hours in the kitchen to make these meals. None requires more than 25 minutes of your time—so the whole working time can be spent listening to the evening news. While many dishes need additional cooking time, you can be doing something else.

Here's the inside scoop on the recipes in this book—diet and denial may start with the same letter, but it ends there. These dishes reflect my exuberance for ingredients and for good-tasting foods. I love to cook because I love to eat.

I love herbs and spices, and start almost all dishes with at least a few cloves of garlic. (For those of you with family and friends who don't like garlic, add some shallots cooked well.) Chile peppers contain almost no calories, but boost flavors in foods immeasurably. They're part and parcel of Southwestern dishes as well as holding a revered place in most Asian cuisines. You'll find them in many recipes in this book.

Perhaps you're new to worrying about the caloric content of food. Stick with me; I'm a pro at it. In fact, this book is the result of one woman's lifelong battle with her hips. The battle has been waged since childhood, and it has certainly been exacerbated by the choice of profession as a food writer and cookbook author. I have a metabolism that should be declared illegal under the Geneva Convention, and I have fought the Battle of the Bulge countless times.

As the founding food editor of *USA Today* in the early 1980s, I had what was perceived by my friends as a "dream job"; I flew around the country eating. Between these forays finding the best gumbo in the Louisiana bayous or the trendiest pizza in Los Angeles, I returned to my home base in Washington, D.C., and starved myself as penance for the most recent caloric transgressions. I lived by a system of "calorie banking." We save calories at lunch to splurge at dinner, or we skip breakfast thinking about the pastries crowning dinner the night before. This might work for the short term; but it's not a healthy way of life.

The trend towards low-calorie cooking in restaurants dates back to the 1970s with the coining of the term "Spa Cuisine." While it accompanied the pounding and prodding at the country's upscale spas, it soon spread to restaurants such as the famed Four Seasons in New York, where the rich (and thin) dined in between spa visits.

What I found while investigating this style of cooking, however, was a combination of elaborate presentation in conjunction with portion control. Remember that even a slice of buttery foie gras can boast a low calorie count if the portion is the size of a thimble.

As a home cook, I had a real aversion to what I term "fondled food." Six snow peas arranged in a starburst pattern might make a pretty picture, but it took way too much time to create and was not filling.

Portion control, the other tenet of early Spa Cuisine, was also not a solution; it left me hungry. The Food and Drug Administration also did not approve of portion control. The FDA definition of "low-calorie" is very clear; it's 120 calories per 100-gram portion of food. That is the standard used for these recipes, with a few exceptions in Chapter 9 for baked goods and desserts. Some of those treats fall into the definition of "reduced-calorie," which is at least 25 percent fewer calories than a standard dish.

My devotion to healthful cooking resulted in the publication of *The Gourmet Gazelle Cookbook* in 1989, for which I won the IACP Cookbook Award. The book was an outgrowth of a business I founded with partners in New York a few years earlier; it was the country's first gourmet take-out shop that sold only nutritionally controlled foods. The assumption was that it was on nights when people were eating at home, or at their desks for lunch, that they wanted food healthier than the usual carry-out could provide.

So that history brings me to this new effort to help you hold the bulge and hold the budget. These are hard times; spa visits are accounted for in few family budgets. But you can do it at home.

Happy eating!

Ellen Brown
Providence, Rhode Island

Acknowledgments

There's only one name on a book, but it takes a team to bring it to fruition. My thanks go to:

Karen Konopelski, my nutritional consultant, for her insights and for allowing me to tap her knowledge as well as her database.

Eugene Brissie, of The Lyons Press, for his support.

Ellen Urban, of The Lyons Press, for her editorial guidance and great humor through the production process.

Jessie Shiers, for her eagle-eyed copyediting.

Tigger and Patches, my furry feline companions, for their hours of snoozing in my office to keep me company.

Introduction

While studies touting the benefits of a low-calorie diet have been around for many decades, it was as recently as February of 2009 that the venerable *New England Journal of Medicine* validated once again that counting calories is the way not only to take off weight, but to keep it off. It's basic chemistry; it's not bells and whistles or magic tricks. And using the delicious recipes in this book is a way to follow this regimen both deliciously *and* economically.

And it appears as a nation we should be paying attention. The Centers for Disease Control and Prevention (CDC) reported that in 2007—the most recent year for which statistics are available—only Colorado had an adult obesity rate of less than 20 percent, with 38 states greater than 25 percent, and 3 states (Alabama, Mississippi, and Tennessee) having the dubious distinction that more than 30 percent of the adult population is obese. If only obesity was an adult problem. Right now more than 12 percent of preschool-age children are already obese, and that figure rises to 17 percent for children aged 6 to 11 and 17.6 percent for adolescents aged 12 to 19.

We have begun to consider calories only in terms of those we take in; however, calories are a measurement of energy and of potential output rather than intake. Calories are burned by every human activity, including lying perfectly still and breathing. The number of calories that an individual will burn during any given task varies according to personal metabolism. It is difficult to determine how many calories each individual should eat in the course of a day to maintain weight and, therefore, to determine what number is needed in order to lose weight.

When the body is using more calories than it is taking in, the necessary energy is taken from the storage of fat cells in our bodies. While that number is individually determined, a rule of thumb is that it takes 3,500 more calories of output than intake in order to lose 1 pound. So eating 500 fewer calories a day or expending an extra 500 calories each day through more vigorous exercise will subtract 1 pound a week, at least in theory.

It's a paradox that while concern about the shape of our shapes is at an all-time high, the American diet continues to be notoriously unhealthful and high in calories. It's not just how many calories we consume in a day, but also which foods comprise those calories that determines whether or not our diet is healthful.

What does not change from person to person is the percentage of calories that should come from fat for a healthy diet. Health authorities are almost unanimous that 30 percent or less of daily calories should come from fat, with 10 percent of those calories from saturated fat—that's the fat found primarily in animal products. So if you're on a 2,000-calorie-a-day eating plan, then it should contain no more than 65 grams of fat, 20 grams or fewer of which are saturated fat.

All fats are a combination of saturated, polyunsaturated, and mono-unsaturated fatty acids. Regardless of the type of fat, they all contain 9 calories per gram, and a gram is a *very* small amount. But fat is an essential nutrient, along with protein, vitamins, and minerals.

You'll notice that all fats—luscious unsalted butter, heady olive oil, and aromatic Asian sesame oil—are used very sparingly in these recipes. While this is touted as a "low-calorie" rather than a "low-fat" cookbook, it's safe to say that you can't control one without controlling the other. Regardless of which oil, there are 120 calories per tablespoon. To put that into perspective, for that same 120 calories you could be eating more than half a cantaloupe or 1 cup of cooked whole-wheat pasta. Which one do you think you'd find more satisfying? In Chapter 2 you'll be reading lots of hints on "skinny cooking," and more tips for maintaining a healthy, low-calorie lifestyle.

While keeping fat in check is important, there's a whole big world of delicious foods that you can—and should—eat on a daily basis. Your body needs more than 40 nutrients on a regular basis to maintain good health, and no single food supplies more than a few of them.

A good rule is that the closer a food is to its raw and natural state, the better it will be for you. Whole grains—including such grains as brown rice, barley, wheat bran, and oat bran—are complex carbohydrates, while refined grains—like white flour and refined sugar—are simple carbohydrates. You want the complex carbohydrates that are also filled with fiber and contain no cholesterol. These whole grains are also high in antioxidants, which help build your immune system.

Carbohydrates are foods composed of some combination of starches, sugar, and fiber; they provide the body with the energy we need for all activities, and they break down into glucose, a sugar our cells use as a universal source of energy. The problem with the refined (or "unhealthy") carbs is that they digest so quickly that they can cause a dramatic elevation in blood sugar, which can lead to weight gain and even to diabetes.

The complex (or "good") carbs digest much more slowly. This keeps your blood sugar and insulin levels from rising and falling too quickly; you'll feel fuller both sooner and for longer.

It's not just whole grains that fall into the "healthy carb" family, it's all the beans, fruits, and vegetables you eat. You should be eating 6 to 11 servings of complex carbohydrates each day, in addition to 3 to 5 servings of vegetables and 2 to 4 servings of fruit. While it varies from food to food, a serving is generally ½ cup; the portion size for meat is 3 ounces, and for cheese it's 1 ounce.

While Americans have eaten too much animal protein in recent decades, protein itself is another essential part of a healthy diet. A complete protein, such as that found in meats, eggs, dairy, poultry, and fish, is one that contains all 9 essential amino acids. Foods such as beans and rice are incomplete proteins, but if eaten together they become a complete protein. While it used to be mandated that the two complementary proteins had to be eaten at the same meal, nutritional authorities now say that eating them within the same day will accomplish the creation of a complete protein. If following a vegetarian diet, beans, nuts, and soy products are all excellent sources of proteins; however, nuts are also high in calories.

To learn more about healthy eating as advised in the 2005 version of the Dietary Guidelines for Americans from the U.S. Department of Agriculture, visit www.mypyramid.gov.

As we age, there's another potential benefit to maintaining a low-calorie lifestyle—improving memory. Dr. Veronica Witte and colleagues from the University of Münster in Germany recently published findings from a study that indicated that middle-aged people who slash the calories in their diet by 30 percent were better able to remember lists of words than people who stuck to their normal routine. It's the first experiment to show that cutting calories may *improve* human memory at a time when memory shortens for a majority of people.

Fifty healthy people between the ages of 52 and 68 were put on a variety of diets—including low-calorie and low-carbohydrate; there was also a control group that did not change their diet. After three months, the blood samples showed that the low-calorie participants had a lower level of the hormone insulin, and those who showed the greatest improvement in memory also had the largest falls in insulin. While this study is both small and preliminary, if you needed another inducement to take the low-cal road, that may be it!

Getting going on a low-calorie way of life is not difficult. Here are some tips to help you get started:

- **Become a human calorie counter.** There are countless inexpensive books on the market that contain calorie counts for ingredients as well as brand-name supermarket foods and foods eaten away from home. There's also a wealth of information for free online. Get a source, and familiarize yourself with it.

- **Start reading food labels.** Almost all contain the number of calories. And pay attention to the serving size represented by that number.

- **Keep a food diary.** While this does not have to be a permanent part of your life, when starting a low-calorie way of eating it helps you to curb the "mindless munching" that thwarts us all. Write down everything that goes into your mouth, including the cookie you ate because they were being given out for free at the supermarket or the few pieces of candy you popped while waiting in line at the bank—just because they were there. Did you spread butter on your cracker? Did you add extra dressing to your salad? These are all the pitfalls that keeping the diary will point out.

It's much easier to keep track of your calories when you cook the food yourself, and what you'll learn reading—and cooking from—this book is how far your limited food budget can stretch. Your wallet grows fatter while your waist grows smaller.

The goal of *$3 Low-Calorie Meals,* as well as other books in the *$3 Meals* series, is an ambitious one; this small amount of money—less than the cost of a large fast food burger or a slice of gourmet pizza—is for your *whole meal!*

That includes the greens for your tossed salad, and the pasta or rice you cook to enjoy all the gravy from a stew. And it includes a sweet treat for dessert. So unlike many books that promise cost-conscious cooking, this book really means it.

In addition to eating wonderfully, you'll also be eating more healthfully. It may not be by accident that *convenience* and *chemical* start with the same letter. Chemicals are what convenience foods are all about; they are loaded up with them to increase their shelf life, both before and after opening. The recipes in this book don't contain such unhealthy ingredients as trans fats and high fructose corn syrup that can be hidden in processed foods, too.

One of the rules of economical cooking is that the more processed a food is, the more expensive it is. These recipes are made with foods that are ingredients; at one time they grew from the earth, walked upon it, or swam in its waters. The most processing that has taken place is the milk of animals transformed into natural cheeses. So when you're cooking from *$3 Low-Calorie Meals,* you're satisfying your body as well as your budget.

Not only for your body, but also for the planet, it is beneficial to use organic ingredients whenever possible. While organics used to be priced higher than conventional products, that is no longer necessarily the case. Most major supermarket chains, and mass retailers such as Wal-Mart, now carry extensive lines of organic ingredients, both fresh and shelf-stable. So buying organic is now a choice open to all—regardless of food budget.

The term was vague until 2001, when the U.S. Department of Agriculture set standards that clearly defined the meaning of "organic," both in terms of the food and the farming practices.

Organic agriculture prohibits the use of most synthetic fertilizers and pesticides, sewer sludge fertilizers, genetic engineering, growth hormones, irradiation, antibiotics, and artificial ingredients. In modern times antioxidants in our bodies have had to work even harder to combat the ravages of environmental pollutants, and organic farming does not add to those factors.

When the word organic is used in relation to meats, eggs, and dairy products, it means that the animals have not been given drugs or growth hormones, and they have been kept in conditions that allow for regular exercise and humane treatment.

In terms of saving the earth, the agricultural practices used for organic farming are environmentally friendly. Soil fertility and crop nutrient management must be done to improve soil conditions, mini-mize erosion, and prevent contamination of crops. Farmers must use crop rotation methods and fertilize with composted animal manure and plant materials rather than chemicals. Pests are controlled by traps rather than chemical sprays, and plastic mulches are forbidden.

In these recipes, I've made a few ingredient compromises to trim costs; however, these shortcuts trim preparation time, too. For my series of *$3 Meals* books I've used bottled lemon and lime juice in recipe development rather than freshly squeezed juices from the fruits them-selves; I discovered it took a bit more juice to achieve the flavor I was after, but with the escalated cost of citrus fruits this was a sacrifice that I chose to make. The same is true with vegetables; many of these recipes call for cost-effective frozen vegetables rather than fresh. For vegetables such as the chopped spinach added to a soup or casserole, or the peas added to many recipes, using frozen vegetables doesn't affect the finished dish.

I've also limited the range of herbs and spices specified to a core group of less than a dozen. There's no need to purchase an expensive dried herb that you may never use again. If you grow fresh herbs, please feel free to substitute them at the rate of 1 tablespoon of a chopped fresh herb for each 1 teaspoon of a dried herb. While I adore fresh herbs, a small bunch in most supermarkets is double the cost of a dozen eggs—and that can serve as the protein for six people's dinner.

On the other hand, there are standards I will never bend. I truly believe that unsalted butter is so far superior to margarine that any minimal cost savings or savings of saturated fat grams from using mar-garine is not worth the trade-down in flavor. Good quality Parmesan cheese, freshly grated when you need it, is another ingredient well worth the splurge. You use very little of it, because once grated it takes up far more volume than in a block, and its innate flavor is far superior.

You'll also find that the dishes in *$3 Low-Calorie Meals* offer a wide range of flavors, and are dishes that are satisfying to the soul as well as to the stomach. You definitely won't feel like a bunny eating these recipes, but you will be lighter and more agile as a result.

Chapter 1:
Saving Money at the Supermarket

Forget that image you have of the lady wearing the hairnet and the "sensible shoes" in line at the supermarket digging through what seems to be a bottomless pit of tiny pieces of paper looking for the right coupon for this or that. Clipping coupons—in case you haven't heard—is *cool.* And it should be. At any given moment there are *billions of dollars* of coupons floating around out there, according to the folks at www.grocerycouponguide.com, one Web site on the growing list of similar sites dedicated to helping you save money.

And not only is it becoming easier to access these savings, you're a Neanderthal if you don't. The fact that you're reading this book—and will be cooking from it—shows that you care about trimming the size of your grocery bill as well as trimming the size of your waistline—or maintaining both where they are right now. So it's time to get with the program, and that's what you're going to learn to do in this chapter.

Most of the tips are specific to food shopping; this *is* a cookbook. But there are also hints for saving money in other segments of your budget. It's all coming out of the same wallet.

Next to housing and auto expenses, food is our major annual expense, as it is around the world. The fact that Americans spend about a 12 percent chunk of disposable income on food still remains the envy of most people living in the industrialized world. Just across the border in Canada the figure is 14 percent, while in Mexico it is more than 25 percent.

PLAN BEFORE YOU SHOP

The most important step to cost-effective cooking is to decide logically and intelligently what you're going to cook for the week. That many sound simple, but if you're in the habit of deciding when you're leaving work at the end of the day, chances are you've ended up with a lot of high-calorie frozen pizza or greasy Chinese carry-out. While this section on how to plan is very detailed, it really takes but minutes to compile your master plan once you've gotten in the habit.

First, look at the week, and what activities are listed. How many nights will you actually be home? Are there guests invited for any meals?

How about the kids? Do they have activities that mean that the family won't be eating dinner together? Is there a sporting event on television that everyone will want to see, so eating may be on laps instead of a table? These are all questions to ponder before putting pen to paper.

The next step is to shop in your own house first. Look and see what's still in the refrigerator, and how that food—which you've already purchased and perhaps also cooked—can be utilized.

Now look and see what foods you have in the freezer. Part of savvy shopping is stocking up on foods when they're on sale; in fact, sales of free-standing freezers have grown by more than 10 percent during the past few years, while sales of all other major appliances have gone down. And with good reason—a free-standing freezer allows you to take advantage of sales. Especially foods like boneless, skinless chicken breasts—the low-calorie diet's best friend—go on sale frequently and are almost prohibitive in price when they're not on sale. You should always have a cache of them ready to cook, for the recipes in this book as well as recipes that are more indulgent.

But preparing food for the freezer to ensure quality is important. Never freeze meats, poultry, or seafood in the supermarket wrapping alone. To guard against freezer burn, double wrap food in freezer paper or place it in heavy resealable plastic bags. Mark the purchase date on raw food, and the date when frozen on cooked items, and use them within three months. Keep a list taped to the front of the freezer so you don't forget about foods. Always try to use the foods that have been frozen for the longest time first.

The recipes in this book use less meats, fish, and poultry than many in other cookbooks; these high-priced foods are also higher in calories. Therefore, it's important to repackage meats into smaller packages than those you buy, too. Scan recipes and look at the amount of the particular meat specified; that's what size your packages destined for the freezer should be.

Also, part of your strategy as a cook is to do it only a few nights a week; that means when you're making a recipe that can be doubled—like a pasta sauce or stew—you make larger batches and freeze a portion. Those meals are "dinner insurance" for nights you don't want to cook. Those are the nights that you previously would have brought in the bucket of chicken or the pizza, and spent more money for more calories by far.

The other factor that enters into the initial planning is to look at your depletion list, and see what foods and other products need to be purchased. A jar of peanut butter or a bottle of dishwashing liquid might not factor into meal plans, but they do cost money—so they have to be factored into your budget. Some weeks you might not need many supplies, but it always seems to me that all of the cleaning supplies seem to deplete the same week.

STRATEGIES FOR SHOPPING

It's a new world out there. You're going to the supermarket and you're going to buy what's on your list. Here's the first rule: stick to that list. Never go shopping when you're hungry; that's when non-essential treats wind up in your basket.

The next time you are at the market, have a pad and pen with you. Take notes of what is located where, such as "baking supplies (flour, sugar, chocolate chips) in aisle 2," and create a master form for your shopping list according to the layout of your market. Divide a sheet of paper into three columns, starting with the meats, fish and other protein, and then make listings for dairy products and shelf-stable pantry items by aisle number. After a few times, this system becomes so familiar that you will probably not be referring to your master guide.

Supermarkets are almost all designed to funnel traffic into the produce section first; that is the last place you want to shop. Begin with the proteins, since many items in other sections of your list relate to the entrees of the dinners you have planned. Once they are gathered, go through and get the shelf-stable items, then the dairy products (so they will not be in the cart for too long) and end with the produce. Using this method, the fragile produce is on the top of the basket, not crushed by the gallons of milk.

The last step is packing the groceries. If your grocery store gives you the option of packing them yourself, place items stored together in the same bag. That way all of your produce can go directly into the refrigerator, and canned goods destined for the basement will be stored in one trip.

COUPON CLIPPING 101

It's part art, it's part science, and it all leads to more money in your wallet. Consider this portion of the chapter your Guerilla Guide to Coupons.

There's more to it than just clipping them. Of course, unless you clip them or glean them from other channels (see some ideas below) then you can't save money. So that's where you're going to start—but, trust me, it's just the beginning.

Every Sunday newspaper (as long as they still exist) is a treasure-trove of coupons. I found a $5 off coupon for a premium cat food my finicky cats liked in a local paper, which cost 50 cents. It was worth it to buy four copies of the paper; I spent $2 but I then realized a net savings of $18 on the cat food.

The first decision you have to make is how you're going to organize your coupons. They are myriad ways, and each has its fans. It's up to you to decide which is right for you, your family, and the way you shop.

- **Arrange the coupons by aisle in the supermarket** if you only shop in one store consistently.

- **Arrange them by category of product** (like cereals, cleaning supplies, dairy products, etc.) if you shop in many stores.

- **Arrange coupons alphabetically** if you have coupons that you use in various types of stores beyond the grocery store.

- **Arrange coupons by expiration date.** Coupons are only valid for a certain time period; it can be a few weeks or a few months. And part of the strategy of coupon clipping is to maximize the value, which frequently comes close to the expiration date. Some of the best coupons are those for "buy one, get one free." However, when the coupon first appears the item is at full price. But what about two weeks later when the item is on sale at your store? Then the "buy one, get one free" can mean you're actually getting four cans for the price of one at the original retail price.

Storage systems for keeping coupons are as varied as methods of organizing them. I personally use envelopes, and keep the stack held together with a low-tech paper clip. I've also seen people with whole wallets and tiny accordion binders dedicated to coupons. If you don't have a small child riding on the top of the cart, another alternative is to get a loose-leaf notebook with clear envelopes instead of pages.

BARGAIN SHOPPING 2.0

Every grocery store has weekly sales, and those foods are the place to start your planning for new purchases; that's how you're saving money beyond using coupons. And almost every town has competing super-market chains that offer different products on sale. It's worth your time to shop in a few venues, because it will generate the most savings. That way you can also determine which chain offers the best store brands, and purchase them while you're there for the weekly bargains. Here are other ways to save:

- **"Junk mail" may contain more than junk.** Don't toss those Val-pack and other coupon envelopes that arrive in the mail. Look through them carefully, and you'll find not only coupons for food products, but for many services, too.

- **Spend a stamp to get a rebate.** Many large manufacturers are now sending out coupon books or cash vouchers usable in many stores to customers who mail in receipts demonstrating that they have purchased about $50 of products. For example, Procter & Gamble, the country's largest advertiser and the company for which the term "soap opera" was invented, is switching millions of dollars from airwaves to these sorts of promotions.

- **Find bargains online.** It's difficult for me to list specific Web sites because they may be defunct by the time you're reading this book, but there are hundreds of dollars worth of savings to be culled by printing coupons from Web sites, and for high end organic prod-ucts, it's the only way to access coupons. Ones I use frequently are www.couponmom.com and www.coupons.com, and I also look for the coupon offers on such culinary sites as www.epicurious .com and www.foodnetwork.com. You will find coupons there, some tied to actual recipes. Also visit manufacturers' Web sites, which offer both coupons and redemption savings.

- **Find coupons in the store.** Look for those little machines project-ing from the shelves; they usually contain coupons that can be used instantly when you check out. Also, don't throw out your receipt until you've looked at it carefully. There are frequently coupons printed on the back. The cashier may also hand you other small slips of paper with your cash register receipt; most of them are coupons for future purchases of items you just bought. They may be from the same brand or they may be from a competing brand. Either way, they offer savings.

- **Stock up on cans.** Even if you live in a small apartment without a basement storage unit, it makes sense to stock up on canned goods when they're on sale. The answer is to use every spare inch of space. The same plastic containers that fit under your bed to hold out of season clothing can also become a pantry for canned goods.

- **Shuffle those cards.** Even if I can't convince you to clip coupons, the least you can do for yourself to save money is take the five minutes required to sign up for store loyalty cards; many national brands as well as store brands are on sale only when using the card. While the current system has you hand the card to the cashier at the checkout, that will be changing in the near future. Shopping carts will be equipped with card readers that will generate instant coupons according to your purchasing habits. I keep my stack of loyalty cards in the glove box of my car; that way they don't clutter my purse but I always have them when shopping.

- **Get a bargain buddy.** There's no question that supermarkets try to lure customers with "buy one, get one free" promotions, and sometimes one is all you really want. And those massive cases of paper towels at the warehouse clubs are also a good deal—if you have unlimited storage space. The answer? Find a bargain buddy with whom you can split large purchases. My friends and I also swap coupons we won't use but the other person will. Going back to my example of the cat food savings, there were dog food coupons on the same page, so I turned them over to a canine-owning friend.

LEARNING THE ROPES

The well-informed shopper is the shopper who is saving money, and the information you need to make the best purchasing decision is right there on the supermarket shelves. It's the shelf tag that gives you the cost per unit of measurement. The units can be quarts for salad dressing, ounces for dry cereal, or pounds for canned goods. All you have to do is look carefully.

But you do have to make sure you're comparing apples to apples and oranges to oranges—or in this example, stocks to stocks. Some stocks are priced by the quart, while others are by the pound.

- **Check out store brands.** Store brands and generics have been improving in quality during the past few years, and according to *Consumer Reports,* buying them can save anywhere from 15 percent to 50 percent. Moving from a national brand to a store brand is a personal decision, and sometimes money is not the only factor. For example, I have used many store brands of chlorine bleach, and have returned to Clorox time and again. But I find no difference between generic corn flakes and those from the market leaders. Store brands can also be less expensive than national brands on sale—and with coupons.

- **Compare prices within the store.** Many foods—such as cold cuts and cheeses—are sold in multiple areas of the store, so check out those alternate locations. Sliced ham may be less expensive in a cellophane package shelved with the refrigerated foods than at the deli counter.

- **Look high and low.** Manufacturers pay a premium price to shelve products at eye level, and you're paying for that placement when you're paying their prices. Look at the top and bottom shelves in aisles like cereal and canned goods. That's where you'll find the lower prices.

- **Buy the basics.** When is a bargain not a bargain? When you're paying for water or you're paying for a little labor. That's why even though a 15-ounce can of beans is less expensive than the same quantity of dried beans (approximately a pound), you're still better off buying the dried beans. One pound of dried beans makes the equivalent of four or five cans of beans. In the same way, a bar of Monterey Jack cheese is much less expensive per pound than a bag of grated Monterey Jack cheese. In addition to saving money, the freshly grated cheese will have more flavor because cheese loses flavor rapidly when grated. And pre-cut and pre-washed vegetables are truly exorbitant.

WASTE NOT, WANT NOT

We're now going to start listing exceptions to all the rules you just read, because a bargain isn't a bargain if you end up throwing some of it away. Remember that the goal is to waste nothing. Start by annotating your shopping list with quantities for the recipes you'll be cooking. That way you can begin to gauge when a bargain is a bargain. Here are other ways to buy only what you need:

- **Don't overbuy.** Sure, the large can of diced tomatoes is less per pound than the smaller can. But what will you do with the remainder of the can if all you need is a small amount? The same is true for dairy products. A half-pint of heavy cream always costs much more per ounce than a quart, but if the remaining 3 cups of cream will end up in the sink in a few weeks, go with the smaller size.

- **Sometimes bigger isn't better.** If you're shopping for snacks for a young child, look for the *small* apples rather than the giant ones. Most kids take a few bites and then toss the rest, so evaluate any purchases you're making by the pound.

- **Ring that bell!** You know the one; it's always in the meat department of supermarkets. It might take you a few extra minutes, but ask the real live human who will appear for *exactly* what you want; many of the recipes in *$3 Low-Calorie Meals* specify less than the weight of packages you find in the meat case. Many supermarkets do not have personnel readily available in departments like the cheese counter, but if there are wedges of cheeses labeled and priced then someone is in charge. It might be the deli department or the produce department, but find out who it is and ask for a small wedge of cheese if you can't find one the correct size.

- **Check out the bulk bins.** Begin buying from the bulk bins for shelf-stable items, like various types of rice, beans, dried fruits, and nuts. Each of these departments has scales so you can weigh ingredients like dried mushrooms or pasta. If a recipe calls for a quantity rather than a weight you can usually "eyeball" the quantity. If you're unsure of amounts, start by bringing a 1-cup measure with you to the market. Use the scoop in the bin to fill the measuring cup rather than placing it directly into the bag or container. One problem with bulk food bags is that they are difficult to store in the pantry; shelves were made for sturdier materials. Wash out plastic deli containers or even plastic containers that you bought containing yogurt or salsa. Use those for storage once the bulk bags arrive in the kitchen. Make sure you label your containers of bulk foods both at the supermarket and if you're transferring the foods to other containers at home so you know what they are, especially if you're buying similar foods. Arborio and basmati rice look very similar in a plastic bag, but they are totally different grains and shouldn't be substituted for each other.

- **Shop from the salad bar for tiny quantities.** There's no question that supermarkets charge a premium price for items in those chilled bins in the salad bar, but you get exactly what you need. When to shop there depends on the cost of the item in a larger quantity. At $4 per pound, you're still better off buying a 50-cent can of garbanzo beans, even if it means throwing some of them away. However, if you don't see how you're going to finish the $4 pint of cherry tomatoes, then spend $1 at the salad bar for the handful you need to garnish a salad.

SUPERMARKET ALTERNATIVES

All of the hints thus far in this chapter have been geared to pushing a cart around a supermarket. Here are some other ways to save money:

- **Shop at farmers' markets.** I admit it; I need a 12-step program to help me cure my addiction to local farmers' markets. Shopping *al fresco* on warm summer days turns picking out fruits and vegetables into a truly sensual experience. Also, you buy only what you want. There are no bunches of carrots; there are individual carrots sold by the pound. The U.S. Department of Agriculture began publishing the *National Directory of Farmers' Markets* in 1994, and at that time the number was fewer than 2,000. That figure has now doubled. To find a farmers' market near you, go to www.ams.usda.gov/farmersmarkets. The first cousins of farmers' markets for small quantities of fruits are the sidewalk vendors in many cities. One great advantage to buying from them is that their fruit is always ripe and ready to eat or cook.

- **Shop at ethnic markets.** If you live in a rural area this may not be possible, but even moderately small cities have a range of ethnic markets, and that's where you should buy ingredients to cook those cuisines. All the Asian condiments used in *$3 Low-Calorie Meals* are far less expensive at Asian markets than in the Asian aisle of your supermarket, and you can frequently find imported authentic brands instead of U.S. versions. Even small cities and many towns have ethnic enclaves, such as a "Little Italy"; each neighborhood has grocery stores with great prices for those ingredients and the fresh produce used to make the dishes, too.

- **Shop alternative stores.** Groceries aren't only at grocery stores; many "dollar stores" and other discount venues stock shelf-stable items. Also, every national brand of drugstore—including CVS and Walgreen's—carries grocery products, and usually has great bargains each week. In the same way that food markets now carry much more than foods, drug stores stock thousands of items that have no connection to medicine. Those chains also have circulars in Sunday newspapers, so check them out—even if you're feeling very healthy.

- **Shop online.** In recent years it's become possible to do all your grocery shopping online through such services as Peapod and Fresh Express. While there is frequently a delivery charge involved, for housebound people this is a true boon. If you really hate the thought of pushing the cart, you should explore it; it's impossible to make impulse buys. There are also a large number of online retailers for ethnic foods, dried herbs and spices, premium baking chocolate, and other shelf-stable items. Letting your cursor do the shopping for these items saves you time, and many of them offer free shipping at certain times of the year.

THAT FRUGAL FRAME OF MIND

In addition to all the tips listed above, you've got to get into a frugal frame of mind. You're out to save money on your food budget, but not feel deprived. You're going to be eating the delicious dishes in this book.

Think about where your food budget goes other than the grocery store. The cost of a few "designer coffee" treats at the local coffee shop is equal to a few dinners at home. Couldn't you brew coffee and take it to work rather than spend $10 a week at the coffee cart? And those cans of soft drinks in the vending machine are four times the cost of bringing a can from home. But do you really need soft drinks at all? For mere pennies you can brew a few quarts of iced tea, which has delicious flavor without chemicals.

Bringing your lunch to work does increase your weekly supermarket tab, but it accomplishes a few good goals. It adds funds to the bottom line of your total budget, and it allows you to control what you're eating—and when. While you may think that your choices for lunch are low calorie, chances are you're kidding yourself, but you won't be kidding your body. That lean little salad comes with a packet of traditional dressing that may contain upwards of a few hundred calories! That's more than many of the entrees in this book.

If you have a pressured job, chances are there are days that you end up eating from snack food vending machines or eating fast food at your desk. If you bring your lunch, you know what it will be—even if you don't know when. Almost every office has a microwave oven, so lunch can frequently be leftovers from a dinner the night or two before, so the extra cost is minimal.

So now that you're becoming a grocery guru, you can move on to find myriad ways to save money on your grocery bill while eating wonderfully. That's what *$3 Low-Calorie Meals* is all about.

Chapter 2:
Taking the Low (Calorie) Road to Health

As we're devoting more attention to changing our eating habits so the choice of low-calorie foods becomes second nature, our cooking habits have to change, too, so that preparing healthier foods also becomes second nature. In this chapter you'll learn tips for both.

MODIFYING YOUR COOKING METHODS

I promise that by making even small steps in your cooking, you can significantly cut back on the calories in your diet. While the savings may not be that great at any individual meal, the cumulative effect of altering your style of cooking can substantially improve your health—and your waistline.

Our cooking habits exist on both conscious and unconscious levels. We began to absorb cooking techniques watching as children in the kitchen. Who doesn't remember the beating of butter and sugar together until it reached that ethereal stage of "light and fluffy" as the foundation of countless goodies? When cookbooks and cooking classes were virtually unknown, generations of cooks learned only by oral instruction, and passed on the basic techniques of cooking rich food suitable for farmers and laborers. Healthy cooking methods are a very recent phenomenon in Western society, although part of many Asian cuisines, and it's often difficult to reconcile them with our favorite traditional foods.

You may have an old recipe in your files—a family favorite—that you know is not healthful. Yet, it's like an old friend, whose flaws you overlook and whose delights you enjoy. This chapter will help you modify your cooking habits to produce dishes with fewer calories than before, and will give you tips on how to continue enjoying favorite dishes while lowering their calories.

MEASURING SUCCESS

Learn to look before you cook, always keeping an eye to how you can cut back on the fat—and its corollary calories—in a dish. It's a good idea to read through a recipe in advance, rather than attempting to change it while concentrating on the mechanics of its successful completion. Annotate the recipe with the substitutions you plan to make and then make notes about the results.

Measuring rather than guessing is the place to begin. Try this test right now: pour what you think is 2 tablespoons of oil into a large skillet. Or, without looking at the wrapper for guidance, slice off 1 teaspoon of butter. My bet is—if you're like me and most cooks—what you poured or sliced is a larger quantity. Use only enough butter or oil to coat the bottom of a pan lightly. One or two tablespoons of fat is all that is necessary to prevent the foods from sticking to the pan when you're sautéing onions, garlic, or other vegetables. If a recipe calls for more, cut back.

At first, your cream soup may taste "thin" made with whole milk instead of heavy cream, and your banana bread may not have the identical texture when it's made with 1/3 of the amount of nuts specified in your grandmother's recipe. But by learning how to substitute lower-fat products for ones you have been using, you can preserve the basic nature of your old favorites. As your palate generally adjusts to lighter foods, those old favorites will still taste good to you—just slightly different from your childhood memories.

Don't expect your palate to adjust immediately to some of these suggested substitutions; take it a step at a time. Cut back on the cream by 1/3, for example, and the next time make it 2/3. Our palates have the ability to appreciate infinite flavors, but they take time to evolve.

DAIRY PRODUCTS

Dairy products are perhaps the largest category of foods open to substitutions. There are very few recipes that absolutely require the use of heavy cream or unsalted butter in large amounts. The calorie and fat savings are incredible: heavy cream has 800 calories per cup, half-and-half has 300 calories per cup, and whole milk has 150 calories per cup.

In recipes such as cream soups, part of the classic French tradition, substitute whole milk for the cream specified. If you want the soup to have a "creamier" consistency, thicken it slightly with 1 teaspoon of arrowroot or cornstarch mixed with 2 tablespoons of cold water. Or puree some of the vegetables in the soup to thicken its texture.

Another genre of recipes specifying heavy cream is mousses, which call for whipped cream either to make them light or to hold their shape.

In place of pure heavy cream, use ⅓ of the amount and whip it extremely stiff; then fold in ⅔ plain nonfat yogurt. The resulting mixture replicates the texture of whipped cream. To mold a mousse with less cream, soften 1 tablespoon of unflavored gelatin in 2 tablespoons of water for 10 minutes and then heat this mixture over low heat until the granules have dissolved. Fold the gelatin into your mousse base.

Sour cream, as luscious as it may be, is another high-calorie culprit, so whenever possible, substitute plain nonfat or low-fat yogurt. While sour cream is 493 calories per cup, nonfat plain yogurt is 137 calories per cup! The difference between whole buttermilk and 3.5 percent low-fat buttermilk is 464 versus 150 calories a cup. Another alternative is to substitute soy milk, which is between 80 and 120 calories per cup, depending on the brand.

Changing the cheeses you use, and the amount of cheese, can create foods with a creamy, cheesy taste and a fraction of the calories, and this is also where measuring becomes important. You frequently see the term "au gratin," and that means topped with cheese or some combination of cheese, breadcrumbs, and fat just before serving. Just by putting the cheese on top, rather than in the dish, you'll taste the wonderful flavor of cheese but save hundreds of fat calories since the cheese is only on the surface. For example, 1 tablespoon of Parmesan cheese has only 23 calories and delivers lots of flavor! Also, use the low-fat versions of cheeses—including mozzarella, ricotta, and cheddar.

LEANER MEATS AND POULTRY

Ground meats offer the butcher a chance to use the fatty, gristly scraps of meat left over from leaner cuts. When buying ground meats, let your eye rather than your wallet be your guide. The lighter the tone of the ground beef, the more fat is present, and the more calories that meat will have. I specify extra-lean ground beef in these recipes, which will be more expensive than packages of ground chuck and will also have a less rich flavor. But the extra cost is a justifiable savings when you compare the fat content, and also the more expensive ground beef does not shrink as much when cooked. Always choose ground beef that is more than 90 percent lean; I've seen it as high as 95 percent lean at some markets.

While that's the bad news about price and value, here's the good news—standard and choice meat is leaner than the more expensive prime. The U.S. Department of Agriculture has eight grades for beef, and part of what designates prime-grade meat is the marbling of fat within the tissue. While it's slightly tougher, choice-grade meat is substantially leaner. For example, a 3-ounce piece of broiled prime beef tenderloin contains 270 calories and 20 grams of fat, while the same size piece of choice-grade beef contains 216 calories and 13 grams of fat. If you can't find the choice grade, ask your butcher to order it for you. Ethnic markets are often a good source.

The calories and fat saved by eating skinless poultry are equally impressive. A 3.5-ounce serving of chicken breast with the skin attached has 197 calories and 8 grams of fat, while the same meat with the skin removed has 165 calories and 4 grams of fat.

If you want to prove to yourself how much saturated fat is contained in poultry skin, cut a piece of chicken skin into small pieces and render the fat in a small saucepan. The skin from just one chicken breast will render 2 to 3 tablespoons of saturated fat.

IT'S ALL IN THE PROPORTION—AND PORTION

It's not just fast-food restaurants that have been "super-sizing" meals to contribute to Americans' weight gains; cookbooks have a role as well. A recent study in the *Annals of Internal Medicine* compared the recipes for eighteen classic dishes from the original edition of the *Joy of Cooking* published in 1936 and the same dishes in the 2006 edition. Overall, the scientists found, the changes in both ingredients and serving size led to a 35.2 percent increase in the calories per serving. In all fairness, the 2006 edition also includes a chapter on nutrition by Dr. Walter Willett, chairman of the nutrition department at the Harvard School of Public Health. However, the trend over the years—and editions—was for more high-caloric meats and less low-caloric vegetables.

In general, 3 to 4 ounces of red meat (about the size of a pack of cards) or 5 to 6 ounces of poultry should be considered a serving. Fill out the remainder of your meal with vegetables, whole grains, and fruits. For meat and poultry, try to use dry rather than wet cooking methods. Marinating foods and then grilling, broiling, or baking them allows much of the fat within the fiber to be released and drip into the cooking pan; the marinade ingredients also impart flavor with a fraction of the calories of a sauce.

On a cold winter night, however, there are few foods as comforting as a plate of steaming stew. Braised dishes should be made either the day before you want to serve them or in the morning of that day. Chill all braised meat dishes prior to serving, to remove any saturated fat that has seeped from the meat during the cooking process. It will appear as a solid layer on the top of the casserole, which can be scraped off and discarded.

MODIFYING BAKED GOODS

In sweets and baked goods, many of the modification rules for the courses that precede them apply. You can usually cut back by 1 whole egg in a cake and substitute 2 additional egg whites. You can also glaze baked goods with egg whites rather than whole eggs.

I've found that most baked goods will not suffer if the sugar and fat are reduced by 25 percent. While baking is more precise than most cooking, and there are certain chemistries involved, few recipes are intolerant of some reductions. When creaming the butter and sugar for a cake, for example, a few tablespoons less will only subtly change the resulting product, while the savings in calories and fat are substantial.

Nuts, an ingredient in many baked goods, are very high in calories. Walnut pieces, for example, have 770 calories and 74 grams of fat per cup. While the texture might be slightly different, you will achieve the same nutty taste by cutting the amount of nuts in half, toasting them in a 350°F oven for 5 minutes to release their flavor and crisp them, and then substituting 1 tablespoon of walnut oil for other fat in the recipe.

For pastries and pies, roll the dough as thinly as possible and bake it for a shorter period of time. A one-crust pie, rather than the standard double-crust pie, is a tremendous fat and calorie saver. Another idea is to use uncooked rolled oats with a small amount of butter to give baked desserts a crunchy topping instead of making streusel crumbs with flour and a large amount of fat.

PROCESSED FOODS

The recipes in this book call for almost no processed foods; they're more expensive and you are paying for the convenience. Just remember the "3 C's" to avoid when shopping, because convenience, cost, and chemicals go hand in hand.

I know it takes time and energy to read labels, and it's not exactly compelling reading. But it's important if you want to reduce the number of calories in your diet, and labels are now far easier to read than they were a few decades ago because of advances by the FDA.

What is important to notice, in addition to the calorie count, is what serving size is specified. That's where manufacturers think they're tricking you into a false sense of caloric security. Perhaps you think a package would feed two people, but then you note that the number of servings is listed as five. Calculate the true calorie count accordingly. That's how much you'll really be eating.

Examine processed foods carefully, especially meats. Look for the reduced-fat, reduced-sodium cold cuts—different companies now produce these options for salami, bologna, and ham. Rather than purchasing turkey or chicken roll, which is injected with a high-sodium stock and contains fat, look in the delicatessen for roasted turkey breast, lean baked ham, or lean freshly roasted beef.

Only buy water-packed tuna, which is easy to do because it's now the norm rather than the exception. A 3.5-ounce portion of tuna packed in water and drained has 127 calories and less than 1 gram of fat, as compared with 197 calories and 8 grams of fat for the fish packed in oil. If oil-packed tuna is the only option, allow it to drain for several minutes and then pat it with paper towels to remove as much oil as possible.

In the same way, if you don't make your own salad dressings, drain some of the oil from commercial salad dressings (you'll find it floating on top) and dilute them with water or chicken stock.

Frozen fruits are another category in which an informed choice can make a difference. Buy only fruits that are packed without sugar syrup, and the calorie counts will be almost equivalent to those of fresh fruit. For example, 1 cup of frozen strawberries has 52 calories, while the same amount packed in sugar syrup has 245 calories.

LOW-CALORIE COOKING TECHNIQUES

We call it stir-frying when cooking Asian dishes in uniformly small pieces, and the method's European cousin is called a sauté. When sautéing, the pieces can be larger and can be left alone in the pan without attention for longer periods of time. Both cooking methods, if done correctly, are inherently low-calorie and also preserve a lot of the nutritional content of vegetables because they remain crisp-tender and the nutrients have not leached out into the cooking water. While the two techniques are related, there are enough differences that I've discussed them in separate sections.

Stir-Frying

For stir-frying, advance planning, speed, and control are the keys to success. The ancient Chinese invented stir-frying as one of their more than fifty methods of food preparation. However, many recipes are now utilizing the technique for non-Asian dishes. It's quick, requires little fat, and leaves food with the crisp-tender texture we enjoy today.

Because the final cooking is a quick process, when stir-frying begins the food must be sitting in bowls or dishes placed within arm's reach, ready to be cooked. Cut all pieces of the same ingredient the same size, have your seasonings at hand, and make sure that partial pre-cooking required—such as blanching green beans—has already been done.

Another aspect of Asian presentation that makes the dishes attractive is how the food is sliced, and there's no difference in the time it takes for simple or dramatic. The rationale behind both methods below is that these cuts create a larger surface area. And it's contact of the surfaces with the hot pan that produces crisp-tender food the most quickly. Here are the two basic Asian slicing techniques:

- **Slicing on the diagonal.** This is a "no-brainer." Instead of cutting celery ribs or scallions at a right angle, tilt your knife so that the slices are at a 45-degree angle. Your pieces will be longer and more attractive.

- **Roll cutting.** This method is sort of like walking and chewing gum at the same time, but it's hardly difficult. This is especially attractive for round vegetables like carrots and asparagus spears. While cutting on the diagonal, turn the vegetable a quarter turn between slices using your other hand. The pieces will be regularly irregular.

The game plan is that when the dish comes to the table all the ingredients are properly cooked, so there are two options: Either cut food that takes longer to cook into smaller pieces and cook everything at the same time, or start with the longer cooking food and keep adding ingredients according to their decreasing need of time. Both strategies produce good results. Never place too much food in the wok or skillet at one time. The food must be able to be seared on all sides, without steaming from being buried under a layer of food.

While it's possible to adapt many recipes to stir-frying, oil rather than butter should be used. The dairy solids in butter burn at a very low temperature, 250°F, so it can only be added as a flavoring agent once food is cooked. Oil, on the other hand, does not begin to smoke until it is heated to more than 400°F, so it is the better choice. There is no consensus as to what oil to use; that's why I lump them together as "vegetable oil" in the ingredient lists. Peanut, corn, soy, or canola all work well, with canola oil containing the least amount of saturated fat. Olive oil will give the dish a pronounced flavor, and it smokes at too low a temperature to be effective in searing the food. And while they're not commonly found in the supermarket, both coconut oil and palm oil should be avoided because, even though they are vegetable products, they do contain a high amount of saturated fat. Place the wok or skillet over a high flame, and heat it very hot. Sprinkle a few drops of water and listen for the sound of sizzles; if the drops evaporate immediately, the pan is ready. Add the required amount of oil to the pan, and swirl it around gently to coat all sides.

Add the food, and keep it moving in the pan. If stir-frying in a wok, use a wire mesh spoon designed for the job. If stir-frying in a skillet, use a spoon that will reach to all places on the bottom, and with which you can keep food moving. In some recipes, liquid is added and the pan is covered for a brief time. In other recipes, it's fry and eat.

Sautéing

Sauté literally means "to jump" in French. What it means for food is quick cooking with just a little fat over moderate to high heat. You sauté foods all the time and don't even know it. All those times that you cook onions or shallots (with or without garlic) at the beginning of cooking a dish, that's a sauté. The reason for this initial cooking is to soften these ingredients' natural harshness before they're transferred to the finished dish.

Like a stir-fry, a sauté produces a meal in very little time and in one pan. Like broiling, sautéing is reserved for relatively thin and tender pieces of protein. It's not for "stewing meat" that needs both time and moisture to get tender. Nor is it suited to large pieces, because the outer portions would become dry before the interior cooked properly.

As is true with foods for a stir-fry, preparing food is the first step to a great sauté. The pieces of food must be of equal size and thickness so that they cook evenly, regardless of whether it is diced onions or chicken cutlet. Sautéing is not recommended for any pieces of poultry or fish more than ½ inch thick since it is unlikely that the center will be properly cooked before the outside is dried. For meat, the thickness can be up to 1 inch, since most people would want the center to be rare.

The purpose of the fat is to lubricate the pan and keep the food from sticking. The fat selected must be able to reach relatively high temperatures without breaking down or smoking. The best selections are cooking oil or a combination of oil and butter. Foods that are sautéed need room around them, so that they cook from the heat and not from the steam created as juices are released. Also, if too much food is put into the pan at one time it will lower the temperature of the pan so that heat will not be transferred with the proper intensity.

BEHAVIOR FOR LOW-CALORIE EATING

We've now talked about how to modify your cooking to create foods that are lower in calories than you might be making now. But it doesn't stop here. It's *how* you eat as much as *what* you eat that can make a difference. Here are some tips for changing your approach to eating:

- **Purge the pantry.** While it does waste some money, that's money you already spent, so get rid of foods in your pantry and refrigerator that you shouldn't eat; those are the ones to which you'll fall prey when wanting a high-calorie snack. Replace the high-sugar jams with fruit only, and banish white bread in favor of whole-wheat and multi-grain.

- **Keep yourself hydrated.** Women should be drinking 9 cups of fluids a day, and the amount for men is 13 cups. While water and calorie-free beverages (including coffee and tea!) are best, fruit juices and skim milk also count. Keep fruit juices to 8 ounces a day, and only choose brands that are 100 percent fruit juice; "fruit drinks" can be loaded with high fructose corn syrup.

- **Get enough sleep.** Studies show that chronic lack of sleep can actually alter the balance of hormones that generate appetite and make you hungrier, so you eat more. Aim for seven hours of sleep a night.

- **Eat slowly.** It takes time for the brain to learn from the stomach that you're feeling full and satisfied—which is the time to stop eating, regardless of whether there's still food on your plate. So wolfing down food might be good if you're a wolf, but not if you're a human. Take time to chew your food well, and savor the flavors in every bite. The recipes in this book are full of flavor; that compensates for their lean approach.

- **Eat when calm.** Not only can eating when stressed lead to indigestion and heartburn, it also leads to over-eating and not properly enjoying food. Stressed eating includes eating while driving, watching television, or sitting in the movies. If you concentrate on your food, you'll find it more filling.

- **Use smaller plates.** This might sound strange, but because we eat first with our eyes, if we see a fuller plate it becomes more emotionally satisfying. Use what we would term "salad plates" for entrée portions, too.

- **Eat regular meals.** Skipping a meal leads to ravenous hunger, which then leads to over-eating and slows down your metabolism. Even if you're not feeling that hungry, have *something* to eat at a regular meal time—especially in the morning to jump-start your metabolism with breakfast.

- **Start with a starter.** A salad made with one of the low-calorie dressings in Chapter 3 or a small bowl of soup drawn from the recipes in Chapter 4 are part of your low-calorie eating plan. And they're included in the definition of your *$3 Low-Calorie Meals.* So don't skip them; both the bulk of the salad and the volume of the soup make you feel fuller faster.

- **Satisfy that sweet tooth—healthfully.** If there are three foods you should eat when craving something sweet, they're fruit, fruit, and fruit. There's no such thing as a fresh fruit that's "bad for you." But do watch out for dried fruits; they're much higher in calories. If you've got to have a cookie, make it a low-calorie biscotti or meringue rather than a chocolate chip. And for the ultimate "fix," have a few squares from a bar of bittersweet, dark chocolate; it has the most antioxidants.

- **Splurge on "bad foods."** Remember, what you're after is a lifestyle of low-calorie eating. So go ahead and nibble a few potato chips, but remember those calories when you're sitting down to dinner.

- **Question the restaurant server.** Dining out, especially when on a strict food budget, should be a treat in every sense—but not at the expense of your low-calorie eating plan. Go for broiled, grilled, sautéed, or poached food rather than fried, and ask the server for all sauces and dressings on the side. Also, if the portion is large, you don't need to eat it all. Feel free to take the leftovers home! Every restaurant now has "doggie bags," and a lot of us don't have dogs. In fact more than 40 percent of diners ask to take home food remaining on their plate, according to the National Restaurant Association.

If you follow these suggestions, not only will you be saving calories in the course of a day, you'll also be enjoying the sensual potential of food more.

Pear Dressing

Ripe pears, on the market and reasonably priced for much of the year, are what give this dressing its rich, thick texture. Try it on grilled or broiled fish or poultry, too.

Yield: 2 cups | **Active time:** 5 minutes | **Start to finish:** 5 minutes

> 2 ripe pears, peeled, cored, and diced
> 5 tablespoons cider vinegar
> 1 tablespoon Dijon mustard
> 2 tablespoons chopped fresh parsley
> 1 teaspoon herbes de Provence
> Salt and freshly ground black pepper to taste
> 2 tablespoons olive oil

Combine pears, vinegar, mustard, parsley, herbes de Provence, salt, and pepper in a blender or in a food processor fitted with the steel blade. Puree until smooth. Add oil, and blend again. Serve immediately.

Note: The dressing can be prepared up to 2 days in advance and refrigerated, tightly covered. Allow it to sit at room temperature for 30 minutes, and shake well before serving.

Each 2-tablespoon serving contains:
23 calories
15 calories from fat
2 g fat
0 g saturated fat
0 g protein
2 g carbohydrates

Variations:
- Substitute 4 ripe apricots, peeled, for the pears; the taste will be more tangy and less creamy.
- While it will raise the caloric count, add ¼ cup blanched almonds to the dressing.

Balsamic Vinaigrette

In addition to tossed salads, try this as the dressing on cold pasta salads or drizzle it on grilled meat or poultry.

Yield: 1 ¼ cups | **Active time:** 5 minutes | **Start to finish:** 5 minutes

½ cup orange juice
⅓ cup balsamic vinegar
2 tablespoons lemon juice
1 tablespoon Dijon mustard
1 teaspoon Italian seasoning
2 garlic cloves, peeled and minced
Salt and freshly ground black pepper to taste
2 tablespoons olive oil

Combine orange juice, vinegar, lemon juice, mustard, Italian seasoning, garlic, salt, and pepper in a jar with a tight-fitting lid. Shake well, add olive oil, and shake well again. Serve immediately.

Note: The dressing can be prepared up to 2 days in advance and refrigerated, tightly covered. Allow dressing to sit at room temperature for 30 minutes, and shake well before serving.

Each 2-tablespoon serving contains:
40 calories
23 calories from fat
3 g fat
0 g saturated fat
0 g protein
3 g carbohydrates

Variation:
- Substitute lime juice for the lemon juice and 2 tablespoons chili powder for the Italian seasoning, and add 2 tablespoons chopped fresh cilantro to the dressing.

Vinaigrette dressing also makes an excellent marinade for meat, poultry, or seafood. Combine equal parts of dressing and wine in a heavy resealable plastic bag, and add the food to be marinated. Seafood should be marinated for no more than 30 minutes, while poultry can soak for up to 4 hours, and meats up to 6 hours.

Rosemary Vinaigrette

This is what most people taste in their mouths when they order a vinaigrette dressing. It is complexly flavored and tart, with some sharp mustard thrown in.

Yield: 1¼ cups | **Active time:** 5 minutes | **Start to finish:** 5 minutes

 ¼ cup Vegetable Stock (recipe on page 44) or purchased stock
 ¼ cup white wine vinegar
 ¼ cup lemon juice
 2 tablespoons chopped fresh rosemary
 1 tablespoon Dijon mustard
 Salt and freshly ground black pepper to taste
 2 tablespoons olive oil

Combine stock, vinegar, lemon juice, rosemary, mustard, salt, and pepper in a jar with a tight-fitting lid. Shake well, add olive oil, and shake well again. Serve immediately.

Note: The dressing can be prepared up to 2 days in advance and refrigerated, tightly covered. Allow dressing to sit at room temperature for 30 minutes, and shake well before serving.

Each 2-tablespoon serving contains:
30 calories
25 calories from fat
3 g fat
0 g saturated fat
0 g protein
1 g carbohydrates

Variation:
- You can change the dominant herb in this dressing and it changes the whole flavor. Substitute chopped fresh oregano or chopped fresh basil for the rosemary.

Sesame-Ginger Dressing

I make a lot of Asian-inspired food, and this salad dressing made with mild rice vinegar complements those dishes well, since it contains characteristic Asian seasoning and sesame oil. This dressing is perfect to transform leftover cold stir-fried vegetables or leftover rice into an exciting dish.

Yield: 1 cup | **Active time:** 10 minutes | **Start to finish:** 10 minutes

> 2 tablespoons sesame seeds *
> 1 tablespoon grated fresh ginger
> 2 garlic cloves, peeled and minced
> Pinch of crushed red pepper flakes
> ½ cup rice vinegar
> 1 tablespoon dry sherry
> 2 tablespoons reduced-sodium soy sauce
> 1 tablespoon Asian sesame oil *

1. Place sesame seeds in a small skillet over medium heat. Toast for 2–4 minutes, shaking the pan frequently, or until brown. Remove the skillet from the heat.
2. Combine sesame seeds, ginger, garlic, red pepper flakes, vinegar, sherry, and soy sauce in a jar with a tight-fitting lid. Shake well, add oil, and shake well again. Serve immediately.

Note: The dressing can be prepared up to 2 days in advance and refrigerated, tightly covered. Allow dressing to sit at room temperature for 30 minutes, and shake well before serving.

Each 2-tablespoon serving contains:
40 calories
25 calories from fat
3 g fat
0 g saturated fat
1 g protein
2 g carbohydrates

Variations:
- For a sweet-and-sour dressing, add 2 tablespoons hoisin sauce.
- For a much spicier dressing, add 1–2 tablespoons Chinese chile paste with garlic.

* Available in the Asian aisle of most supermarkets and in specialty markets.

Celery Seed Dressing

This is one of my favorite all-American dressings. It's great on coleslaw or any cabbage salad, and can also be used to flavor potato salad.

Yield: 1 cup | **Active time:** 5 minutes | **Start to finish:** 5 minutes

⅓ cup cider vinegar
¼ cup Vegetable Stock (recipe on page 44) or purchased stock
2 tablespoons honey
2 tablespoons orange juice
1 shallot, peeled and minced
2 garlic cloves, peeled and minced
2 teaspoons celery seeds
Salt and freshly ground black pepper to taste
1 tablespoon olive oil

Combine vinegar, stock, honey, orange juice, shallot, garlic, celery seeds, salt, and pepper in a jar with a tight-fitting lid. Shake well, add olive oil, and shake well again. Serve immediately.

Note: The dressing can be prepared up to 2 days in advance and refrigerated, tightly covered. Allow dressing to sit at room temperature for 30 minutes, and shake well before serving.

Each 2-tablespoon serving contains:
37 calories
15 calories from fat
2 g fat
0 g saturated fat
0 g protein
5 g carbohydrates

Unlike the empty calories of refined sugar, honey is loaded with nutrients and is actually sweeter than granulated sugar, so you can use less of it.

Blue Cheese Dressing

Blue cheese is not only a classic dressing for salads, it can also be served at parties as a dip for vegetable crudités. If you're going to be serving all the dressing at once, reserve some of the cheese to sprinkle over the food, too.

Yield: 2 cups | **Active time:** 5 minutes | **Start to finish:** 5 minutes

1¼ cups plain nonfat yogurt
½ cup low-fat buttermilk
½ cup firmly packed crumbled blue cheese
Salt and freshly ground black pepper to taste

Combine yogurt, buttermilk, and blue cheese in a food processor fitted with the steel blade or in a blender. Puree until smooth. Scrape mixture into a bowl, and season to taste with salt and pepper.

Note: The dressing can be made up to 3 days in advance and refrigerated, tightly covered.

Each 2-tablespoon serving contains:

29 calories
12 calories from fat
1 g fat
1 g saturated fat
2 g protein
2 g carbohydrates

Variation:

• Substitute English Stilton or gorgonzola for the blue cheese.

Try this dressing for egg salad or chicken salad. It's as creamy as mayonnaise and has much more flavor for a fraction of the calories.

Yogurt Dill Dressing

Tangy yogurt is a natural pairing with the fresh taste of dill. This dressing is thick enough to be used as a dip with crudités and is also a good substitute for mayonnaise on coleslaw or potato salad.

Yield: 1½ cups | **Active time:** 5 minutes | **Start to finish:** 5 minutes

> 1 cup plain nonfat yogurt
> 2 tablespoons lemon juice
> 1 tablespoon finely chopped onion
> ¼ cup finely chopped cucumber
> ¼ cup minced fresh dill
> Salt and freshly ground black pepper to taste

1. Combine yogurt, lemon juice, onion, and cucumber in a food processor fitted with the steel blade or in a blender. Puree until smooth.
2. Scrape mixture into a bowl, and stir in dill. Season to taste with salt and pepper.

Note: The dressing can be made up to 2 days in advance and refrigerated, tightly covered.

Each 2-tablespoon serving contains:

16 calories
0 calories from fat
0 g fat
0 g saturated fat
1 g protein
3 g carbohydrates

Variations:
- Add ½ cup finely chopped tomato along with the dill.
- Substitute chopped fresh basil for the dill.

> For an even thicker dressing, drain the yogurt in a sieve placed over a mixing bowl for 20 minutes. Much of the liquid whey will end up in the bowl.

Horseradish Sauce

Like its high-calorie cousin, this sauce is wonderful with any roasted meat, especially beef. The sauce is also incredibly low in calories because horseradish is basically a "free food," although few people would want to eat it in any large quantity.

Yield: 2 cups | **Active time:** 5 minutes | **Start to finish:** 5 minutes

1½ cups plain nonfat yogurt
⅓ cup prepared white horseradish
3 scallions, white parts and 3 inches of green tops, rinsed, trimmed, and chopped
2 tablespoons lemon juice
¼ teaspoon dried thyme
Salt and freshly ground black pepper to taste

Combine yogurt, horseradish, scallions, lemon juice, and thyme in a mixing bowl. Stir well, and season to taste with salt and pepper. Refrigerate until ready to use.

Note: The sauce can be made up to 3 days in advance and refrigerated, tightly covered.

Each 2-tablespoon serving contains:
17 calories
1 calorie from fat
0 g fat
0 g saturated fat
1 g protein
3 g carbohydrates

Variation:
- Substitute ½ cup of bottled chili sauce for ½ cup of the yogurt, and the sauce becomes similar to a remoulade sauce.

Greek Feta Sauce

The essence of a Greek salad is a combination of tomatoes, cucumber, and lettuce tossed in a dressing made with sharp feta cheese. This is also a wonderful topping for grilled fish.

Yield: 1½ cups | **Active time:** 10 minutes | **Start to finish:** 10 minutes

½ cup low-fat feta cheese, diced
¾ cup plain nonfat yogurt
2 tablespoons lemon juice
2 garlic cloves, peeled
2 ripe plum tomatoes, rinsed, cored, seeded, and chopped
¼ cup chopped fresh dill
Salt and freshly ground black pepper to taste

1. Combine feta, yogurt, lemon juice, and garlic in a food processor fitted with the steel blade or in a blender. Puree until smooth.
2. Scrape mixture into a mixing bowl, and stir in tomatoes and dill. Season to taste with salt and pepper, and refrigerate sauce until ready to use.

Note: The sauce can be made up to 3 days in advance and refrigerated, tightly covered.

Each 2-tablespoon serving contains:
29 calories
11 calories from fat
1 g fat
1 g saturated fat
2 g protein
3 g carbohydrates

Variation:
• Substitute 1 tablespoon dried oregano for the dill.

Ginger Mignonette

Traditional mignonette dressing is served in bistros in France with shelled oysters. This version has far more flavor, and it's wonderful drizzled over canned tuna.

Yield: ²/₃ cup | **Active time:** 10 minutes | **Start to finish:** 10 minutes

> ⅓ cup plain rice vinegar
> Salt and freshly ground black pepper to taste
> 1 tablespoon Asian sesame oil *
> 2 teaspoons grated fresh ginger
> 1 scallion, white part only, rinsed, trimmed, and thinly sliced
> 1 small jalapeño or serrano chile, seeds and ribs removed, and finely chopped

Combine vinegar, salt, and pepper in a jar with a tight-fitting lid, and shake well. Add oil, ginger, scallion, and chile, and shake well again.

Note: The sauce can be made up to 3 days in advance and refrigerated, tightly covered. Bring it back to room temperature before serving.

Each 2-tablespoon serving contains:
33 calories
25 calories from fat
3 g fat
0 g saturated fat
0 g protein
1 g carbohydrates

Variation:
• Substitute 1 teaspoon wasabi powder for the chile pepper.

* Available in the Asian aisle of most supermarkets and in specialty markets.

Cilantro Honey Mustard Sauce

I use this sauce on any cold meat, and its heady flavor is so much more appealing than just using mustard. The aromatic sesame oil lends its own fragrance as well as flavor.

Yield: 1 cup | **Active time:** 5 minutes | **Start to finish:** 5 minutes

$\frac{1}{2}$ cup Dijon mustard
3 tablespoons honey
1 tablespoon Asian sesame oil *
$\frac{1}{4}$ cup chopped fresh cilantro
Salt and freshly ground black pepper to taste

Combine mustard, honey, and sesame oil in a small bowl. Whisk until smooth. Stir in cilantro, and season to taste with salt and pepper. Serve immediately.

Note: The sauce can be made up to 3 days in advance and refrigerated, tightly covered. Allow it to sit at room temperature for 30 minutes before serving.

Each 2-tablespoon serving contains:
44 calories
15 calories from fat
2 g fat
0 g saturated fat
0 g protein
6.5 g carbohydrates

* Available in the Asian aisle of most supermarkets and in specialty markets.

Tandoori Indian Sauce

Traditional tandoori chicken is marinated in spiced yogurt before grilling or broiling, but you can achieve the same flavor by using this sauce to top chicken, fish, or meat.

Yield: 1½ cups | **Active time:** 15 minutes | **Start to finish:** 15 minutes

    1 tablespoon vegetable oil
    1 small onion, peeled and finely chopped
    4 garlic cloves, peeled and minced
    2 tablespoons paprika
    1 tablespoon curry powder
    2 teaspoons ground cumin
    1 teaspoon ground ginger
    1 cup plain nonfat yogurt
    ¼ cup lemon juice
    Salt and cayenne to taste

1. Heat oil in a small skillet over medium-high heat. Add onion and garlic, and cook, stirring frequently, for 3 minutes, or until onion is translucent. Add paprika, curry powder, cumin, and ginger, and cook, stirring constantly, for 1 minute. Scrape mixture into mixing bowl.
2. Add yogurt and lemon juice to mixing bowl, and whisk well. Season to taste with salt and cayenne, and serve at room temperature.

Note: The sauce can be made up to 3 days in advance and refrigerated, tightly covered. Bring to room temperature before serving.

Each 2-tablespoon serving contains:
30 calories
15 calories from fat
2 g fat
0.5 g saturated fat
1 g protein
3 g carbohydrates

Creamy Chipotle Sauce

Chipotle chiles are smoked jalapeño chiles that are packed in a thick spicy sauce similar to a hot red pepper sauce—so it should be used sparingly. This sauce is fantastic on any simple entrée when you want a Hispanic flavor.

Yield: 2 cups | **Active time:** 10 minutes | **Start to finish:** 10 minutes

1³/₄ cups plain nonfat yogurt
3 tablespoons lime juice
3 scallions, white parts and 3 inches of green tops, rinsed, trimmed, and chopped
3 garlic cloves, peeled and minced
3 chipotle chiles in adobo sauce, finely chopped
1 teaspoon adobo sauce
Salt to taste

Combine yogurt, lime juice, scallions, garlic, chipotle chiles, and adobo sauce in a mixing bowl. Whisk well, and season to taste with salt. Refrigerate until ready to use.

Note: The sauce can be made up to 3 days in advance and refrigerated, tightly covered.

Each 2-tablespoon serving contains:
21 calories
3 calories from fat
0 g fat
0 g saturated fat
2 g protein
3 g carbohydrates

Variation:
• This makes for an assertive sauce, no question about it. Feel free to cut back on the number of chipotle chiles for a milder flavor.

Herbed Tomato Sauce

This easy-to-make sauce takes the place of purchased marinara sauce in your repertoire, and because it freezes so well you can keep a batch around at all times.

Yield: 2 cups | **Active time:** 15 minutes | **Start to finish:** 1 hour

> 1 tablespoon olive oil
> 1 medium onion, peeled and finely chopped
> 4 garlic cloves, peeled and minced
> 1 carrot, peeled and finely chopped
> 1 celery rib, trimmed and finely chopped
> 1 (28-ounce) can crushed tomatoes
> 2 tablespoons chopped fresh parsley
> 2 teaspoon dried oregano
> 1 teaspoon dried thyme
> 2 bay leaves
> Salt and red pepper flakes to taste

1. Heat olive oil in 2-quart saucepan over medium heat, swirling to coat the pan. Add onion and garlic and cook, stirring frequently, for 3 minutes, or until onion is translucent.
2. Add carrot, celery, tomatoes, parsley, oregano, thyme, and bay leaves. Bring to a boil, reduce heat to low, and simmer sauce, uncovered, stirring occasionally, for 45–50 minutes, or until slightly thickened. Season to taste with salt and red pepper flakes.

Note: The sauce can be made up to 3 days in advance and refrigerated, tightly covered. Bring back to a simmer before serving. It can also be frozen for up to 3 months.

Each ¼ cup serving contains:
40 calories
13 calories from fat
1.5 g fat
0 g saturated fat
2 g protein
7 g carbohydrates

Variation:
- Add ½ green bell pepper, seeds and ribs removed, and finely chopped, to the sauce.

Mexican Tomato Sauce

This sauce is your "utility infielder" whenever you're serving a Mexican or Southwestern dish. Use it on enchiladas, to moisten and flavor tacos, or in place of salsa with chips.

Yield: 2 cups | **Active time:** 15 minutes | **Start to finish:** 30 minutes

> 1 tablespoon olive oil
> 1 small onion, peeled and finely chopped
> 3 garlic cloves, peeled and minced
> 2 tablespoons chili powder
> 1 tablespoon ground cumin
> $\frac{3}{4}$ cup Vegetable Stock (recipe on page 44) or purchased stock
> 1 (15-ounce) can tomato sauce
> 1 (4-ounce) can chopped mild green chiles, drained
> $\frac{1}{4}$ cup chopped fresh cilantro
> Salt and freshly ground black pepper to taste

1. Heat olive oil in a 2-quart heavy saucepan over medium heat, swirling to coat the pan. Add onion and garlic and cook, stirring frequently, for 3 minutes, or until onion is translucent. Reduce the heat to low, stir in chili powder and cumin, and cook, stirring constantly, for 1 minute.
2. Stir in stock, tomato sauce, and green chiles. Whisk well, bring to a boil, and simmer sauce, uncovered, for 15 minutes, stirring occasionally, or until the sauce is reduced by $\frac{1}{4}$.
3. Stir in cilantro, and season to taste with salt and pepper. Serve hot or at room temperature.

Note: The sauce can be made up to 3 days in advance and refrigerated, tightly covered. Bring back to a simmer before serving. It can also be frozen for up to 3 months.

Each $\frac{1}{4}$ cup serving contains:
32 calories
18 calories from fat
2 g fat
0 g saturated fat
0 g protein
4 g carbohydrates

Variation:
- Add 1 jalapeño or serrano chile, seeds and ribs removed, and finely chopped, along with the onion and garlic for a spicier sauce.

Chicken Stock

You'll be amazed at the difference in flavor homemade chicken stock makes to all your dishes. And you'll notice a change in your grocery bill when you can stop buying it!

Yield: 4 quarts | **Active time:** 10 minutes | **Start to finish:** 4 hours

> 6 quarts water
> 5 pounds chicken bones, skin, and trimmings
> 4 celery ribs, rinsed and cut into thick slices
> 2 onions, trimmed and quartered
> 2 carrots, trimmed, scrubbed, and cut into thick slices
> 2 tablespoons whole black peppercorns
> 6 garlic cloves, peeled
> 4 sprigs parsley
> 1 teaspoon dried thyme
> 2 bay leaves

1. Place water and chicken in a large stockpot, and bring to a boil over high heat. Reduce the heat to low, and skim off foam that rises during the first 10–15 minutes of simmering. Simmer stock, uncovered, for 1 hour, then add celery, onions, carrots, peppercorns, garlic, parsley, thyme, and bay leaves. Simmer for 2½ hours.
2. Strain stock through a fine-meshed sieve, pushing with the back of a spoon to extract as much liquid as possible. Discard solids, spoon stock into smaller containers, and refrigerate. Remove and discard fat from surface of stock, then transfer stock to a variety of container sizes.

Note: The stock can be refrigerated and used within 3 days, or it can be frozen for up to 6 months.

Each 1-cup serving contains:
12 calories
1 calorie from fat
0 g fat
0 g saturated fat
0 g protein
3 g carbohydrates

Variation:
• For turkey stock, use the same amount of turkey giblets and necks as chicken pieces.

Beef Stock

While beef stock is not specified as often as chicken stock in recipes, it is the backbone to certain soups and the gravy for stews and roasts.

Yield: 2 quarts | **Active time:** 15 minutes | **Start to finish:** $3\frac{1}{2}$ hours

>   3 pounds beef trimmings (bones, fat) or inexpensive beef shank
>   3 quarts water
>   1 carrot, trimmed, scrubbed, and cut into thick slices
>   1 medium onion, peeled and sliced
>   1 celery rib, trimmed and sliced
>   1 tablespoon whole black peppercorns
>   3 sprigs fresh parsley
>   1 teaspoon dried thyme
>   2 garlic cloves, peeled
>   2 bay leaves

1. Preheat the oven broiler, and line a broiler pan with heavy-duty aluminum foil. Broil beef for 3 minutes per side, or until browned. Transfer beef to a large stockpot, and add water. Bring to a boil over high heat. Reduce the heat to low, and skim off foam that rises during the first 10–15 minutes of simmering. Simmer for 1 hour, uncovered, then add carrot, onion, celery, peppercorns, parsley, thyme, garlic, and bay leaves. Simmer for 3 hours.

2. Strain stock through a fine-meshed sieve, pushing with the back of a spoon to extract as much liquid as possible. Discard solids, and spoon stock into smaller containers. Refrigerate; remove and discard fat from surface of stock.

Note: The stock can be refrigerated and used within 3 days, or it can be frozen for up to 6 months.

Each 1-cup serving contains:
13 calories
1 calorie from fat
0 g fat
0 g saturated fat
0 g protein
3 g carbohydrates

Variation:
- Should you encounter any veal or lamb bones, add them to the stock. However, do not add pork bones.

Seafood Stock

Seafood stock is a great reason to make friends with the head of the fish department of your supermarket. You can arrange in advance to have them save lobster bodies for you if the store cooks lobster meat, or you can purchase them at minimal cost. The same is true with fish bones, if a store fillets the fish on site.

Yield: 2 quarts | **Active time:** 15 minutes | **Start to finish:** $1^3/_4$ hours

> 3 lobster bodies (whole lobsters from which the tail and claw
>   meat has been removed), shells from 3 pounds raw shrimp, or 2
>   pounds bones and skin from firm-fleshed white fish such as hali-
>   but, cod, or sole
> 3 quarts water
> 1 cup dry white wine
> 1 carrot, scrubbed, trimmed, and cut into 1-inch chunks
> 1 medium onion, peeled and sliced
> 1 celery rib, rinsed, trimmed and sliced
> 1 tablespoon whole black peppercorns
> 3 sprigs fresh parsley
> 1 teaspoon dried thyme
> 2 garlic cloves, peeled
> 1 bay leaf

1. If using lobster shells, pull top shell off 1 lobster body. Scrape off and discard feathery gills, then break body into small pieces. Place pieces into the stockpot, and repeat with remaining lobster bodies. If using shrimp shells or fish bones, rinse and place in the stockpot.

2. Add water, wine, carrot, onion, celery, peppercorns, parsley, thyme, garlic, and bay leaf. Bring to a boil over high heat, then reduce the heat to low and simmer stock, uncovered, for $1^1/_2$ hours.

3. Strain stock through a fine-meshed sieve, pushing with the back of a spoon to extract as much liquid as possible. Discard solids, and allow stock to cool to room temperature. Spoon stock into smaller containers, and refrigerate.

Note: The stock can be refrigerated and used within 3 days, or it can be frozen for up to 6 months.

Each 1-cup serving contains:

31 calories

1 calorie from fat

0 g fat

0 g saturated fat

0 g protein

2 g carbohydrates

Variations:

- Substitute tarragon for the thyme.
- Substitute fennel for the celery.

Finding commercial fish and seafood stocks is becoming easier than it was a few years ago. There are also small jars of pastes to reconstitute in many health food stores. And then there's bottled clam juice, which is universally available.

Vegetable Stock

You may think it's not necessary to use vegetable stock if making a vegetarian dish that includes the same vegetables, but that's not the case. Using stock creates a much more richly flavored dish that can't be replicated by increasing the quantity of vegetables cooked in it.

Yield: 2 quarts | **Active time:** 10 minutes | **Start to finish:** 1 hour

- 2 quarts water
- 2 carrots, scrubbed, trimmed, and thinly sliced
- 2 celery ribs, rinsed, trimmed, and sliced
- 2 leeks, white part only, trimmed, rinsed, and thinly sliced
- 1 small onion, peeled and thinly sliced
- 1 tablespoon whole black peppercorns
- 3 sprigs fresh parsley
- 1 teaspoon dried thyme
- 2 garlic cloves, peeled
- 1 bay leaf

1. Pour water into a stockpot, and add carrots, celery, leeks, onion, peppercorns, parsley, thyme, garlic, and bay leaf. Bring to a boil over high heat, then reduce the heat to low and simmer stock, uncovered, for 1 hour.

2. Strain stock through a fine-meshed sieve, pushing with the back of a spoon to extract as much liquid as possible. Discard solids, and allow stock to cool to room temperature. Spoon stock into smaller containers, and refrigerate.

Note: The stock can be refrigerated and used within 3 days, or it can be frozen for up to 6 months.

Each 1-cup serving contains:

15 calories
1 calorie from fat
0 g fat
0 g saturated fat
0 g protein
3.5 g carbohydrates

Chapter 4:

"Little Dishes" for Less than $1

This chapter contains a group of "little dishes." While some of the soups can become a meal if eaten in a larger quantity, these dishes are really intended as appetizers. Or several can be grouped together to become a "grazing meal" of small plates. Enjoying a multi-course meal remains consistent with a low-calorie diet—as long as the courses are chosen carefully. A salad with any of the dressings in Chapter 3 is one option, and any of the dishes in this chapter are another.

Because these are little dishes, they also carry a little price tag. None of these dishes costs more than $1 per serving. This can be factored into your food budget without a stretch, and they'll give you and your tummy much pleasure.

SPEEDY SOUPS

Soup is my favorite way to begin a meal. In summer, chilled soups cool the spirit on a sweltering day as effectively as steaming bowls of soup take the chill from even the most blizzardy winter day. Another advantage to beginning a meal with soup is that it's filling, so the stomach begins to feel satisfied on just a few calories.

The pleasure of soup shouldn't be limited to seated meals. I fill thermos jugs with soup for picnics. Or you can take it to the office for lunch; almost every office now has a microwave oven to reheat hot soups and a refrigerator to keep chilled soups cold.

The majority of the soup recipes in this chapter are quick and easy purees. In my experience there's a finite amount of time that most cooks will spend on any meal, even for a formal party. I would rather put the effort into the main course and have the first course be memorable for its careful blending of flavors, not time-consuming preparation.

You may wonder why there are so many soup recipes that start with the word "cream" or include it in the recipe title. The trick for low-cal soups is that creaminess can be achieved in ways that trick your palate into thinking you're indulging because you're sipping a thick liquid. For the cold soups, most specify plain nonfat yogurt as the dairy product; it provides a sharp dairy note similar to that given by sour cream, but with a fraction of the fat. For hot soups, there's a small amount of light cream or whole milk. The "richness" comes from the high percentage of pureed vegetables, which is a bonus to your diet. You'll also find that these low-calorie soups deliver purer flavors because there's little fat to coat your palate.

The vegetable soups are all written for vegetable stock, but any of them can be made with chicken stock as well. The chicken stock will give them a slightly richer flavor, and the calorie count will remain the same.

APPEALING APPETIZERS

Appetizers should tantalize the taste buds and satisfy the senses with their textures, colors, and flavors. But they should not be filling, or the main dish that follows will not be as eagerly anticipated. The dishes in this chapter meet that definition.

In eating healthfully, one of the most difficult habits to overcome is "mindless munching." These are the snacks that hurt your waistline as well as forming a slow but steady leak in your food budget. This munching extends to parties, and that's why many of the dishes in this chapter are annotated as to how they can be transformed into hors d'oeuvres.

People watching their weight become bored when the only option at a party is the ubiquitous crudités—especially when the dips transform a low-cal nibble to an indulgence. Look at the recipes in Chapter 3; such dishes as the low-cal Blue Cheese Dressing or Yogurt Dill Sauce enliven the veggies without defeating the purpose of eating them.

Curried Carrot Soup

The natural sweetness of carrots, rich in beta-carotene to boost your immune system, is actually accentuated when contrasted with a bit of curry in this quick and easy soup.

Yield: 6 servings | **Active time:** 15 minutes | **Start to finish:** 45 minutes

>   1 tablespoon unsalted butter
>   6 large carrots, peeled and sliced
>   1 medium onion, peeled and sliced
>   ½ large apple, peeled and sliced
>   1½–2 tablespoons curry powder
>   6 cups Chicken Stock (recipe on page 40) or purchased stock
>   ⅓ cup light cream
>   Salt and freshly ground black pepper to taste

1. Melt butter in a 4-quart saucepan over medium heat. Add carrots, onion, and apple, and cook, stirring frequently, for 10 minutes. Stir in curry powder, reduce the heat to low, and cook, stirring constantly, for 1 minute.
2. Raise the heat to medium, and slowly stir in stock. Bring to a boil and simmer over low heat, uncovered, for 20 minutes. Stir in cream, and simmer for 5 minutes, or until carrots are very tender.
3. Puree soup in a food processor fitted with the steel blade or in a blender. Season to taste with salt and pepper, and serve immediately.

Note: The soup can be made up to 2 days in advance and refrigerated, tightly covered. Serve it cold, or reheat over low heat, stirring occasionally.

Each serving contains:
155 calories
66 calories from fat
7 g fat
4 g saturated fat
6 g protein
17 g carbohydrates

Variation:
• Substitute parsnips for the carrots and the soup will be even sweeter.

Southwestern Vegetable Soup

My travels have served as the basis for many dishes, including this one, inspired by the *Sopa Azteca* that is part of traditional Southwestern cooking. It is the specialty of El Mirador in San Antonio, Texas. It's spicy, and while it's cooking, the kitchen is filled with glorious anticipatory aromas.

Yield: 6 servings | **Active time:** 20 minutes | **Start to finish:** 40 minutes

1 tablespoon olive oil
1 medium onion, peeled and diced
2 garlic cloves, peeled and minced
1 (14.5-ounce) can tomatoes, drained
2 teaspoons dried oregano
2 teaspoons dried basil
1 teaspoon ground cumin
4 cups Vegetable Stock (recipe on page 44) or purchased stock
3 tablespoons tomato paste
3 celery ribs, rinsed, trimmed, and sliced
1 small green bell pepper, seeds and ribs removed, and diced
2 medium zucchini, rinsed, trimmed, and sliced
1 large carrot, peeled and diced
1 large redskin potato, scrubbed and cut into ½-inch dice
½ cup canned kidney beans, drained and rinsed
2 (6-inch) corn tortillas
½ cup grated part-skim mozzarella cheese
Vegetable oil spray

1. Heat oil in a 4-quart saucepan over medium-high heat. Add onion and garlic, and cook, stirring frequently, for 3 minutes, or until onion is translucent. Add tomatoes, oregano, basil, and cumin. Cook mixture for 5 minutes over medium heat, stirring frequently.
2. Transfer vegetable mixture to a food processor fitted with the steel blade or to a blender; puree until smooth. Return mixture to the pan, and add stock and tomato paste, stirring well to dissolve tomato paste. Bring to a boil over medium heat.
3. Add celery, green bell pepper, zucchini, carrot, potato, and kidney beans to soup and simmer, uncovered, for 15 minutes, or until the vegetables are cooked through but retain their texture.
4. While soup simmers, preheat the oven to 375°F. Cut each tortilla into 8–10 triangles, and spray lightly with vegetable oil spray. Arrange tor-

tilla wedges on a baking sheet, and bake for 5 minutes, turning once, or until tortilla wedges are crisp. To serve, ladle soup into shallow bowls, and top each serving with tortilla wedges and cheese.

Note: The soup can be made up to 3 days in advance and refrigerated, tightly covered. Reheat it slowly and don't allow it to simmer, or the vegetables will overcook.

Each serving contains:
166 calories
41 calories from fat
4.5 g fat
1 g saturated fat
7 g protein
27 g carbohydrates

Variations:
- Substitute chicken stock for the vegetable stock, and add $\frac{1}{2}$ pound boneless, skinless chicken breast, cut into $\frac{1}{2}$-inch cubes, along with the vegetables. Make sure chicken is cooked through and no longer pink.
- For a spicy dish, add 1–2 jalapeño or serrano chiles, seeds and ribs removed and sliced, to the onion mixture while it's cooking.

The technique of pureeing the base of soups is used extensively in Mexican cooking. It produces a vividly flavored broth that transfers flavor to the vegetables cooked in it.

Lemon Egg Soup

Greek *avgolemono* is rich and velvety from the eggs and refreshing from the lemon juice. Some of the eggs of the traditional soup have been replaced by egg whites to lower the cholesterol count.

Yield: 6 servings | **Active time:** 5 minutes | **Start to finish:** 20 minutes

> 7 cups Chicken Stock (recipe on page 40) or purchased stock
> 1/2 cup orzo
> 1/2 cup lemon juice
> 2 large eggs
> 3 large egg whites
> Salt and freshly ground black pepper to taste

1. Bring stock to a boil in a large covered saucepan over high heat. Add orzo, reduce the heat to low, and simmer, covered, for 10–12 minutes, or until orzo is tender.
2. While soup simmers, whisk lemon juice, eggs, and egg whites. Set aside.
3. When orzo is cooked, turn off the heat and wait until the bubbling has stopped. If you are using an electric stove, remove the pot from the burner. Stir soup with a spoon for 30 seconds. Whisk lemon-egg mixture into hot soup, and immediately cover the pot. Allow the soup to sit undisturbed for 5 minutes. Season to taste with salt and pepper, and serve immediately.

Note: The soup can be made up to 2 days in advance, and refrigerated, tightly covered. Be very careful when reheating it so that it does not come to a boil, or the eggs will curdle.

Each serving contains:
190 calories
47 calories from fat
5 g fat
1.5 g saturated fat
13 g protein
22 g carbohydrates

Variation:
- Add 1/2 pound boneless, skinless chicken breast, cut into 1/2-inch dice, to the soup along with the orzo. Cook until the chicken is cooked through and no longer pink.

Spiced Acorn Squash Soup

This is a traditional American soup, with a hint of bourbon and spices. For this recipe, butternut squash can substitute for the acorn squash.

Yield: 6 servings | **Active time:** 15 minutes | **Start to finish:** 1¾ hours

>3½ pounds (2 medium) acorn squash
>2 cups Vegetable Stock (recipe on page 44) or purchased stock
>2 tablespoons chopped fresh parsley
>2 tablespoons molasses
>2 tablespoons bourbon
>¼ teaspoon ground cinnamon
>Pinch of freshly grated nutmeg
>1 cup whole milk
>Salt and freshly ground black pepper to taste

1. Preheat the oven to 400°F, and line a baking pan with aluminum foil.
2. Bake squash for 1 hour, or until the flesh is tender when probed with a sharp meat fork, turning occasionally during baking. Cut squash in half, discard seeds, and scrape flesh from shell. Cut flesh into 2-inch chunks.
3. Combine squash, stock, parsley, molasses, bourbon, cinnamon, and nutmeg in a 4-quart saucepan. Bring to a boil over medium heat and simmer, partially covered, for 20 minutes.
4. Puree soup in a food processor fitted with the steel blade or in a blender. Return soup to the pan, and add milk. Bring to a boil over medium heat, stirring frequently, and simmer over low heat for 5 minutes. Season to taste with salt and pepper, and serve immediately.

Note: The soup can be made up to 2 days in advance and refrigerated, tightly covered. Reheat it over low heat, covered, stirring occasionally.

Each serving contains:
167 calories
15 calories from fat
2 g fat
1 g saturated fat
4 g protein
36 g carbohydrates

Variation:
- Substitute hoisin sauce, rum, and Chinese five-spice powder for the molasses, bourbon, cinnamon, and nutmeg.

Cream of Celery Soup with Tarragon

Tarragon is an elegant herb with a slight anise, or licorice, flavor. This soup is subtly seasoned, and the rice used for thickening creates a luscious texture.

Yield: 6 servings | **Active time:** 10 minutes | **Start to finish:** 55 minutes

> 4 cups (about ²/₃ bunch) celery, rinsed, trimmed, and sliced
> 3 ¹/₂ cups Vegetable Stock (recipe on page 44) or purchased stock
> ¹/₃ cup white rice
> 2 teaspoons dried tarragon
> ¹/₂ cup whole milk
> Salt and freshly ground black pepper to taste

1. Combine celery, stock, rice, and tarragon in a 4-quart saucepan. Bring to a boil over high heat, stirring occasionally. Reduce the heat to low, and simmer soup, partially covered, for 30 minutes.
2. Puree soup in a food processor fitted with the steel blade or in a blender. Return soup to the pan, stir in milk, and simmer 2 minutes. Season to taste with salt and pepper, and serve immediately.

Note: The soup can be made up to 2 days in advance and refrigerated, tightly covered. Reheat it over low heat, covered.

Each serving contains:
69 calories
8 calories from fat
1 g fat
0 g saturated fat
2 g protein
13 g carbohydrates

Variations:
- Substitute sliced raw fennel for the celery to accentuate the flavor of the tarragon.
- Substitute ¹/₄ cup chopped fresh dill for the tarragon.

Honeydew Gazpacho

This quick puree has the same refreshing quality as the cucumber, mint, and yogurt *raita* used as a fire extinguisher for Indian curries. These ingredients are melded with the subtle sweetness of the melon, and the pale green color is a tonic for a summer day.

Yield: 6 servings | **Active time:** 15 minutes | **Start to finish:** 2¼ hours, including 2 hours to chill

> 6 cups diced ripe honeydew melon
> ⅓ cup distilled white vinegar
> 3 tablespoons chopped fresh mint
> 2 cups sliced celery
> 1 medium onion, peeled and diced
> 2 small cucumbers, peeled, seeded, and diced
> 1 cup plain nonfat yogurt
> Salt and freshly ground black pepper to taste
> 6 fresh mint sprigs for garnish (optional)

1. Combine honeydew melon, vinegar, mint, celery, onion, and cucumbers in a food processor fitted with the steel blade or in a blender. Puree until smooth; this may have to be done in batches.
2. Stir in yogurt, and season to taste with salt and pepper. Refrigerate until cold, at least 2 hours. Garnish each serving with a mint sprig, if using.

Note: The soup can be made up to 2 days in advance and refrigerated, tightly covered. Stir it well before serving.

Each serving contains:
120 calories
5 calories from fat
0.5 g fat
0 g saturated fat
4.5 g protein
26 g carbohydrates

Variation:
- Substitute ¼ cup firmly packed fresh cilantro leaves for the mint.

Golden Gazpacho

This bright orange soup has an almost sweet and sour flavor profile from the luscious ripe melon and carrots contrasted with the vinegar and scallions. It's a great variation on the Spanish prototype.

Yield: 6 servings | **Active time:** 15 minutes | **Start to finish:** 2¼ hours, including 2 hours to chill

 4 cups diced ripe cantaloupe
 1 large carrot, peeled and sliced
 2 small cucumbers, peeled, seeded, and sliced
 8 scallions, white parts only, rinsed, trimmed, and sliced
 ⅔ cup cider vinegar
 1 cup orange juice
 2 tablespoons lemon juice
 Salt and freshly ground black pepper to taste

1. Combine cantaloupe, carrot, cucumbers, scallions, vinegar, orange juice, and lemon juice in a food processor fitted with the steel blade or in a blender. Puree until smooth; this may have to be done in batches.
2. Season to taste with salt and pepper. Refrigerate until cold, at least 2 hours.

Note: The soup can be made up to 2 days in advance and refrigerated, tightly covered. Stir it well before serving.

Each serving contains:
83 calories
4 calories from fat
0.5 g fat
0 g saturated fat
2 g protein
18 g carbohydrates

Variation:

- For a spicier soup, add 1–2 jalapeño or serrano chiles, seeds and ribs removed, to the ingredients.

Selecting melons is never easy because they have such a hard rind. A general rule is to look at the stem end. It should smell sweet and be flat rather than indented. An indentation is a sign that the melon was pulled off the vine before it was ripe, at which time it comes off easily.

Guacamole Soup

Remember, there's no such thing as a "bad food"; the trick is to use delicious foods that are high in calories in moderation as flavoring agents rather than as the starring players. That's the role that buttery avocado plays in this refreshing soup.

Yield: 6 servings | **Active time:** 15 minutes | **Start to finish:** 2¼ hours, including 2 hours to chill

SOUP

1 ripe avocado
1 small onion, peeled and chopped
¼–½ teaspoon hot red pepper sauce, or to taste
2 tablespoons chopped fresh cilantro
2 tablespoons canned chopped mild green chiles, drained
1½ cups plain nonfat yogurt
2 cups Vegetable Stock (recipe on page 44) or purchased stock
Salt and freshly ground black pepper to taste

GARNISH

2 (6-inch) corn tortillas
3 ripe plum tomatoes, rinsed, cored, seeded, and chopped
Vegetable oil spray

1. Peel and stone avocado, and cut into 1-inch cubes. Combine avocado, onion, red pepper sauce, cilantro, chiles, yogurt, and stock in a food processor fitted with the steel blade or in a blender. Puree until smooth; this may have to be done in batches.
2. Season to taste with salt and pepper. Refrigerate until cold, at least 2 hours. Press a sheet of plastic wrap directly into surface of soup to prevent discoloration.
3. While soup chills, preheat the oven to 375°F. Cut each tortilla into 8–10 triangles, and spray lightly with vegetable oil spray. Arrange tortilla wedges on a baking sheet, and bake for 5 minutes, turning once, or until tortilla wedges are crisp. Set aside.
4. To serve, ladle the soup into chilled bowls. Top each serving with a few tortilla strips and a spoonful of diced tomatoes.

Note: The soup can be made up to 2 days in advance and refrigerated, tightly covered. Stir it well before serving.

Each serving contains:
115 calories
36 calories from fat
4 g fat
1 g saturated fat
5 g protein
16 g carbohydrates

Variation:
- For a spicier soup, add 1–2 jalapeño or serrano chiles, seeds and ribs removed, to the ingredients.

In addition to eating avocado in moderation due to its calorie count, it's also an expensive food in most parts of the country. So don't fret if an avocado you thought was ripe turns out not to be. Rub the cut surfaces with mayonnaise, push it back together, and leave it to further ripen at room temperature.

Vichyssoise

Vichyssoise, actually an American invention despite the French name, is the grandma of all cold summer soups. The combination of delicate leeks and onions with creamy potatoes can't be beaten.

Yield: 6 servings | **Active time:** 15 minutes | **Start to finish:** $2^3/_4$ hours, including 2 hours to chill

> 2 tablespoons unsalted butter
> 4 leeks, white parts and 2 inches of light green tops, trimmed, chopped, and rinsed well
> 1 small onion, peeled and chopped
> 1 pound boiling potatoes, peeled and thinly sliced
> 6 cups Chicken Stock (recipe on page 40) or purchased stock
> $^3/_4$ cup plain nonfat yogurt
> Salt and freshly ground black pepper to taste
> 6 tablespoons chopped chives for garnish

1. Melt the butter in a 4-quart saucepan over medium heat. Add leeks and onion, and cook, stirring frequently, for 3 minutes, or until onion is translucent.
2. Add potatoes and stock, and bring to a boil over high heat. Reduce the heat to low, and simmer soup, partially covered, for 25 minutes, or until potatoes are tender.
3. Puree soup in a food processor fitted with the steel blade or in a blender. Stir in yogurt, and season to taste with salt and pepper. Refrigerate until cold, at least 2 hours. To serve, ladle soup into bowls, sprinkling each serving with chopped chives.

Note: The soup can be made up to 2 days in advance and refrigerated, tightly covered. Stir it well before serving.

Each serving contains:
225 calories
51 calories from fat
6 g fat
3 g saturated fat
9 g protein
35 g carbohydrates

Variation:

- Omit the yogurt, and increase the chicken stock by $3/4$ cup. Instead of pureeing the soup, mash some of it with a potato masher and serve it hot.

> You can always substitute finely chopped green scallion tops for chives in any recipe. It's rare that you ever use a whole scallion, so they frequently go to waste.

Dilled Cream of Cucumber Soup

Aromatic dill and delicate cucumber are natural partners. While classic cream of cucumber soup is made with a high-fat cream sauce, the yogurt in this version not only lowers the calories, it speeds up the preparation.

Yield: 6 servings | **Active time:** 15 minutes | **Start to finish:** 2¾ hours, including 2 hours to chill

> 1 tablespoon unsalted butter
> 2 large or 3 small cucumbers, peeled, halved lengthwise, seeded, and sliced
> ¼ cup chopped fresh dill, divided
> 4 cups Vegetable Stock (recipe on page 44) or purchased stock
> 1 cup plain nonfat yogurt
> Salt and freshly ground black pepper to taste
> 6 fresh dill sprigs (optional)

1. Melt butter in a 4-quart saucepan over medium heat. Add cucumber and ½ of dill. Cook, stirring occasionally, for 5 minutes.
2. Add stock, and bring to a boil over high heat. Reduce the heat to low, and simmer soup, partially covered, for 25 minutes, or until cucumbers are soft.
3. Puree soup in a food processor fitted with the steel blade or in a blender. Stir in yogurt and remaining dill, and season to taste with salt and pepper. Refrigerate until cold, at least 2 hours. To serve, ladle soup into bowls and top with dill sprigs, if using.

Note: The soup can be made up to 2 days in advance and refrigerated, tightly covered. Stir it well before serving.

Each serving contains:
68 calories
17 calories from fat
2 g fat
1 g saturated fat
4 g protein
10 g carbohydrates

Variation:
• Substitute fresh chopped basil or oregano for the dill.

Cream of Zucchini Soup with Basil

This thick soup is a natural for summer, when both zucchini and fresh basil are plentiful in the markets, if not in your garden or on your terrace.

Yield: 6 servings | **Active time:** 15 minutes | **Start to finish:** 2³/₄ hours, including 2 hours for chilling

1 tablespoon unsalted butter
1 small onion, peeled and chopped
2 pounds small zucchini, rinsed, trimmed, and thinly sliced
3 cups Vegetable Stock (recipe on page 44) or purchased stock
½ cup firmly packed fresh basil leaves
½ cup light cream
1 cup plain nonfat yogurt
Salt and freshly ground black pepper to taste
6 fresh basil sprigs for garnish (optional)

1. Melt the butter in a 4-quart saucepan over medium heat. Add onion and cook, stirring frequently, for 3 minutes, or until onion is translucent.
2. Add zucchini and stock, and bring to a boil over high heat. Reduce the heat to low, and simmer soup, partially covered, for 20 minutes, or until zucchini is soft.
3. Stir in basil, and puree soup in a food processor fitted with the steel blade or in a blender. Stir in cream and yogurt, and season to taste with salt and pepper. Refrigerate until cold, at least 2 hours. To serve, ladle soup into bowls and top with basil sprigs, if using.

Note: The soup can be made up to 2 days in advance and refrigerated, tightly covered. Stir it well before serving.

Each serving contains:
133 calories
72 calories from fat
8 g fat
5 g saturated fat
5 g protein
12 g carbohydrates

Variation:
- For a more intensely flavored soup, add 2 garlic cloves, peeled and minced, and sauté the garlic with the onions.

Chinese Eggplant Compote

This method of baking the eggplant eliminates the need for the large amounts of salt and oil specified in most eggplant recipes. The Szechwan spicing is inspired by a dish I enjoyed many years ago at the late Barbara Tropp's China Moon Café in San Francisco. It's also a wonderful party hors d'oeuvre; it can be served on cucumber slices or thin toasts.

Yield: 6 servings | **Active time:** 10 minutes | **Start to finish:** 3 hours, including 2 hours to chill

> 2 (1-pound) eggplants
> 4 scallions, white parts and 3 inches of green tops, rinsed, trimmed, and chopped
> 2 garlic cloves, peeled and minced
> ¼–½ teaspoon Chinese chile oil *
> 2 tablespoons reduced-sodium soy sauce
> 1 tablespoon balsamic vinegar
> 1 tablespoon granulated sugar
> 1 tablespoon Asian sesame oil *
> 3 cups shredded lettuce

1. Preheat the oven to 400°F, and line a baking sheet with aluminum foil. Prick eggplants with a sharp meat fork, and place them on the baking sheet.
2. Bake eggplants for 40–50 minutes, turning them after 20 minutes, or until eggplants are uniformly soft. Remove eggplants from the oven. They will look brown and will deflate like punctured balloons. When cool enough to handle, cut off tops and peel away skin with your fingers. Drain any liquid that seeps out by shaking pulp in a sieve, and chop flesh either by hand or in a food processor fitted with the steel blade, using on-and-off pulsing.
3. Combine scallions, garlic, chile oil, soy sauce, vinegar, sugar, and sesame oil in a mixing bowl, and stir well to dissolve sugar. Stir in eggplant, and chill well, at least 2 hours. To serve, arrange lettuce on a small plate and mound the eggplant in the center.

Note: The eggplant can be made up to 2 days in advance and refrigerated, tightly covered.

* Available in the Asian aisle of most supermarkets and in specialty markets.

Each serving contains:
83 calories
26 calories from fat
3 g fat
0 g saturated fat
3 g protein
14 g carbohydrates

Variation:
- Omit the chile oil for a milder dish.

Eggplants have male and female gender, and the males are preferable because they are less bitter and have fewer seeds. To tell a male from a female, look at the stem end. The male is rounded and has a more even hole, and the female hole is indented.

Mushrooms Stuffed with Spinach and Feta

Stuffed mushrooms never go out of style, and sharp, low-fat feta cheese becomes the flavor secret in the bright green spinach filling. These are not only the perfect cocktail party hors d'oeuvre, you can also serve them as a vegetable to glamorize simple entrees as well as serving them as an appetizer.

Yield: 6 servings | **Active time:** 15 minutes | **Start to finish:** 25 minutes

18 large fresh mushrooms
2 tablespoons unsalted butter
2 garlic cloves, peeled and minced
1/4 cup finely chopped onion
1 (10-ounce) package frozen chopped spinach, thawed
2 tablespoons chopped fresh parsley
1/2 teaspoon dried thyme
1 tablespoon lemon juice
1/2 cup crumbled low-fat feta cheese
Salt and freshly ground black pepper to taste

1. Preheat the oven to 375°F, and line a baking sheet with aluminum foil.
2. Wipe mushrooms with a damp paper towel, twist out stems, and trim stems. Set caps aside, and finely chop stems in a food processor fitted with the steel blade, using on-and-off pulsing.
3. Heat butter in a 12-inch skillet over medium heat. Add mushroom stems, garlic, and onion, and cook, stirring frequently, for 7–10 minutes, or until vegetables are soft.
4. Place spinach in a colander, and press with the back of a spoon to remove as much liquid as possible. Add spinach to the pan, and cook for 3 minutes. Add parsley, thyme, lemon juice, and feta. Mix until smooth, and remove the pan from the heat. Season filling to taste with salt and pepper.
5. Stuff mushroom caps with spinach mixture, and arrange on the baking sheet. Bake for 8–10 minutes, or until the mushrooms are cooked. Serve hot or at room temperature.

Note: You can fill the mushrooms up to 1 day in advance, and refrigerate them, tightly covered. Or, you can bake them up to 4 hours in advance, and keep them at room temperature. They are much better if not reheated.

Each serving contains:
158 calories
45 calories from fat
5 g fat
3 g saturated fat
13 g protein
15 g carbohydrates

Variation:
- Substitute goat cheese for the feta.

Contrary to popular belief, the ancient Greeks and Romans did not cultivate mushrooms; they merely encouraged wild ones to grow. It was not until the eighteenth century, when Olivier de Serres was agronomist to French King Louis XIV, that mushroom cultivation began in Europe.

Phyllo Egg Rolls

These crispy, delicate rolls have all the textural qualities of a traditional egg roll—a crunchy vegetable filling flavored with Asian tidbits—yet the thin phyllo dough creates a crispy wrapper with virtually no fat.

Yield: 6 servings | **Active time:** 25 minutes | **Start to finish:** 35 minutes

1 celery rib, rinsed, trimmed, and cut into fine julienne

1/4 medium red onion, peeled and cut into fine julienne

4 scallions, white parts and 3 inches of green tops, rinsed, trimmed, and cut into fine julienne

2 1/4 cups shredded green cabbage

1 tablespoon reduced-sodium soy sauce

1 tablespoon medium sherry

1 teaspoon rice vinegar

1 tablespoon Asian sesame oil *

1 tablespoon grated fresh ginger

2 garlic cloves, peeled and minced

2 tablespoons chopped fresh cilantro

3/4 cup bean sprouts, rinsed and cut into 1-inch lengths

6 sheets phyllo dough, thawed

Vegetable oil spray

1. Preheat the oven to 375°F, line a baking sheet with aluminum foil, and grease the foil with vegetable oil spray.
2. Combine celery, onion, scallions, and cabbage in a mixing bowl. Combine soy sauce, sherry, and vinegar in a small cup, and stir well.
3. Heat oil in a wok or large skillet over high heat. Add ginger and garlic, and stir-fry, stirring constantly, for 30 seconds, or until fragrant. Add vegetables, and stir-fry for 2 minutes, or until slightly cooked but still crisp. Add liquids, and stir-fry for 1 minute. Remove the wok from the stove, and stir in cilantro and bean sprouts. Set aside.
4. Carefully separate 1 sheet of phyllo, and place about 3/4 cup of vegetable filling in the center of one of the shorter ends of the rectangle. Fold the sides around the filling to enclose it, and then roll phyllo into an egg roll. Place egg rolls on the prepared baking sheet seam side down.
5. Spray rolls lightly with vegetable oil spray, and bake for 10–12 minutes, or until golden brown. Cut in half on the diagonal, and serve immediately.

* Available in the Asian aisle of most supermarkets and in specialty markets.

Note: The egg rolls can be prepared for baking up to 1 day in advance and refrigerated, tightly covered. Add 3–5 minutes to the baking time if chilled.

Each serving contains:
99 calories
31 calories from fat
3 g fat
1 g saturated fat
3 g protein
15 g carbohydrates

Variation:
- Substitute ½ cup chopped cooked chicken or pork for ½ cup of the cabbage.

Phyllo dough, also spelled filo, is an incredibly thin dough used primarily in Greek and Middle Eastern cuisines. The tricks to handling it are to make sure it is totally thawed—it comes frozen—and keep the stack of sheets covered with a damp towel so that they don't dry out.

Chapter 5:

One If By Land . . . Part 1: Chicken and Turkey Entrees

Chicken is to the cook what a blank canvas is to a painter; it's the start of endless possibilities for expression—and in this case the expression is delicious. You'll find recipes for chicken as it's enjoyed around the world—from quick stir-fries from Asia to saucy Italian treats. And there are a few recipes that are so crispy, you'll find it hard to believe they're really low-calorie!

Americans' consumption of chicken more than doubled during the past 30 years, and continues to rise. And it's relatively inexpensive, which is why this is such a long chapter.

Chicken is also a great low-calorie food—as long as the skin is not part of the dish. Ah, that wonderfully crispy skin that you love is just loaded with saturated fat. In fact, the skin from just half a small chicken adds more than 250 calories to a dish—and that's after it's been cooked and much of the fat has rendered out of it.

While you can buy skinless pieces, they are always far more expensive than those with skin attached. Always skin the chicken pieces yourself, and save the skin for making stock. The skin doesn't weigh much in relation to the chicken meat, so what you're paying for is—once again—the processing cost for the company to remove the skin for you.

The leanest part of chicken is the breast. Always stock up when they're on sale and freeze them in packets. I can usually find boneless, skinless chicken breasts for about $2.00 to $2.50 per pound when on sale, and they're more than double that cost at regular price. Take the extra few minutes to trim the breasts, and then pound some thinly as described below. Then freeze them individually wrapped; they take but minutes to thaw that way.

COOK IT CORRECTLY

While rules have been changing for pork in the past few years, chicken must still be cooked to an internal temperature of 170°F to ensure that there's no chance for microorganisms to survive. The best way to test the temperature is to use an instant-read meat thermometer.

When the thickest part of the chicken is probed, the reading should be 170°F. But if you don't want to take the temperature of every piece of chicken, here are the visual signals: The chicken is tender when poked with the tip of a paring knife, there is not a hint of pink even near the bones, and the juices run clear. Always test the dark meat before the white meat. Dark meat takes slightly longer to cook, so if the thighs are the proper temperature, you know the breasts will be fine.

CUTTING WITH CUNNING

Just look at the range of prices for chicken in the supermarket. Those pieces least processed—the whole chickens—are always the lowest in cost per pound. Then there are the legs and thighs or leg quarters, which can sometimes be even less expensive than a whole bird because the precious breast meat is gone.

It is far more economical to purchase a whole chicken, and cut it up yourself, rather than buying one already cut. There are also times that your choice of chicken pieces, such as thighs, aren't available, and you can always cut up a few chickens to glean the parts for that meal, and freeze what's left; another benefit is that you can save the scraps and freeze them to keep you "stocked up" for soups and sauces. Here are some methods of chicken cutting you should know:

- **Cutting up a whole chicken:** Start by breaking back the wings until the joints snap; then use the boning knife to cut through the ball joints and detach the wings. When holding the chicken on its side, you will see a natural curve outlining the boundary between the breast and the leg/thigh quarters. Use sharp kitchen shears to cut along this line. Cut the breast in half by scraping away the meat from the breastbone, and use a small paring knife to remove the wishbone. Cut away the breastbone using the shears, and save it for stock. Divide the thigh/leg quarters by turning the pieces over and finding the joint joining them. Cut through the joint and sever the leg from the thigh.

- **Boning chicken breasts:** If possible, buy the chicken breasts whole rather than split. Pull the skin off with your fingers, and then make an incision on either side of the breastbone, cutting down until you feel the bone resisting the knife. Treating one side at a time, place the blade of your boning knife against the carcass, and scrape away the meat. You will then have two pieces per side—the large fillet, and the small tenderloin. To trim the fillet, cut away any fat. Some recipes will tell you to pound the breast to an even thickness, so it will cook evenly and quickly. Place the breast between two sheets of plastic wrap or waxed paper, and pound with the smooth side of a meat mallet or the bottom of a small, heavy skillet or saucepan. If you have a favorite veal scallop recipe, and want to substitute chicken or turkey, pound it very thin—to a thickness of 1/4 inch. Otherwise, what you are after is to pound the thicker portion so that it lies and cooks evenly. To trim the tenderloin, secure the tip of the tendon that will be visible with your free hand. Using a paring knife, scrape down the tendon, and the meat will push away.

Chicken and Mango Wraps

Sweet, luscious mango along with tangy, fresh tomatoes join the lean chicken breast for these low-calorie wraps done in whole-wheat tortillas. Serve them with a tossed salad to add another vegetable serving to your meal.

Yield: 6 servings | **Active time:** 15 minutes | **Start to finish:** 45 minutes

    1 pound boneless, skinless chicken breast halves
    1/2 cup dry white wine
    2 tablespoons chopped fresh cilantro
    1 tablespoon Dijon mustard
    1 teaspoon ground cumin
    Salt and freshly ground black pepper to taste
    3 ripe plum tomatoes, rinsed, cored, seeded, and diced
    1 ripe fresh mango, peeled and diced
    2 tablespoons Balsamic Vinaigrette (recipe on page 26) or
       purchased low-calorie salad dressing
    6 (8-inch) whole-wheat tortillas

1. Light a charcoal or gas grill, or preheat the oven broiler. Rinse chicken and pat dry with paper towels. Trim chicken of all visible fat, and pound to an even thickness of 1/2 inch between two sheets of plastic wrap.

2. Combine wine, cilantro, mustard, cumin, salt, and pepper in a heavy resealable plastic bag, and mix well. Add chicken to marinade, and marinate for 30 minutes at room temperature, turning the bag occasionally.
3. Remove chicken from marinade, and discard marinade. Grill or broil chicken for 3–4 minutes per side, or until chicken is cooked through and no longer pink. Remove chicken from the grill, and cut into 1-inch cubes.
4. Combine chicken, tomatoes, and mango in a mixing bowl. Sprinkle with balsamic vinaigrette, and season to taste with salt and pepper. Wrap tortillas in plastic wrap, and microwave on High (100 percent power) for 20–30 seconds, or until pliable.
5. To serve, divide mixture into tortillas, and fold over 3 sides to encase filling. Serve immediately.

Note: The filling can be made up to 4 hours in advance and refrigerated, tightly covered.

Each serving contains:
272 calories
42 calories from fat
5 g fat
1 g saturated fat
23 g protein
34 g carbohydrates

Variation:
- Substitute 2 navel oranges, peeled and diced, or 1 cup diced fresh papaya for the mango.

Mangoes have an easy and a hard way to peel them. If you start to peel one and it's difficult to peel, start at the other end.

Oven-Fried Chicken Fingers with Sweet Potato Fries

Think that a low-calorie meal can't include chicken "nuggets?" These are even better, and the sweet potato slices are crispy and crusty, too.

Yield: 6 servings | **Active time:** 25 minutes | **Start to finish:** 40 minutes

3 medium sweet potatoes, peeled and very thinly sliced
Cajun seasoning to taste
1¼ pounds boneless, skinless chicken breast halves
2 large egg whites
½ cup low-fat buttermilk
Salt and freshly ground black pepper to taste
4 cups corn flakes
½ cup all-purpose flour
Vegetable oil spray

1. Preheat the oven to 425°F, line two baking sheets with aluminum foil, and grease the foil with vegetable oil spray.
2. Arrange sweet potatoes on one of the prepared baking sheets, and lightly spray tops of slices with vegetable oil spray. Season slices to taste with Cajun seasoning. Bake for 15–20 minutes, or until crisp and browned.
3. Rinse chicken, and pat dry with paper towels. Trim all visible fat, and cut chicken into ½-inch-thick slices against the grain. Place slices between 2 sheets of plastic wrap, and pound to an even thickness of ¼ inch.
4. Combine egg whites, buttermilk, salt, and pepper in a mixing bowl, and whisk until smooth. Crush corn flakes to crumbs in a food processor fitted with the steel blade, using on-and-off pulsing; alternately, place them in a heavy resealable plastic bag and crush them with the flat side of a meat mallet or the bottom of a small skillet. Place crumbs on a sheet of aluminum foil or on a plate.
5. Place chicken slices in a heavy plastic bag with flour, and shake to coat slices. Remove chicken, and shake over the sink or a garbage can to remove excess flour.
6. Dip each chicken slice in the egg mixture, and press into crumbs. Arrange chicken on the prepared pan, and spray it lightly with vegetable oil spray.
7. Bake slices for 7–10 minutes, or until cooked through and no longer pink. Serve immediately, accompanied by sweet potato fries.

Note: The chicken can be prepared for baking up to 6 hours in advance and refrigerated, tightly covered.

Each serving contains:
211 calories
12 calories from fat
1 g fat
0 g saturated fat
25 g protein
24 g carbohydrates

Variations:
- Add 2 tablespoons Dijon mustard to the egg mixture.
- Add 2 tablespoons Italian seasoning to the crumb mixture.
- Add 3 tablespoons chili powder to the crumb mixture.

> The reason why buttermilk is frequently used in marinades and recipes is that the lactic acid is a natural food tenderizer.

Low-Cal Crispy Chicken

You don't need the chicken skin, high in unhealthy saturated fat, to enjoy crispy chicken. This can be made in minutes. Substitute skinless thighs if you like dark meat more than white meat.

Yield: 6 servings | **Active time:** 10 minutes | **Start to finish:** 55 minutes

> 6 (6-ounce) skinless chicken breasts, with bones
> 2 large egg whites
> ³/₄ cup plain nonfat yogurt
> 2 garlic cloves, peeled and minced
> 1 tablespoon herbes de Provence
> Salt and freshly ground black pepper to taste
> ¹/₂ cup cracker crumbs (from your favorite cracker)
> 1¹/₂ cups rice cereal, such as Rice Krispies
> Vegetable oil spray

1. Preheat the oven to 400°F, line a baking sheet with aluminum foil, and grease the foil with vegetable oil spray. Rinse chicken and pat dry with paper towels.
2. Combine egg whites, yogurt, garlic, herbes de Provence, salt, and pepper in a mixing bowl, and whisk well. Combine cracker crumbs and rice cereal in a heavy resealable plastic bag, and crush with the flat side of a meat mallet or the bottom of a small skillet; the rice cereal should retain some texture. Place crumb mixture on a sheet of aluminum foil or on a plate.
3. Dip chicken pieces in the yogurt mixture, and then place them into crumbs, patting crumbs on both sides. Arrange chicken on the prepared pan, and spray chicken with vegetable oil spray.
4. Bake for 45–55 minutes, or until chicken is cooked through and no longer pink, and an instant-read thermometer registers 170°F. Serve immediately.

Note: The chicken can be prepared for baking up to 6 hours in advance and refrigerated, tightly covered.

Each serving contains:

251 calories

24 calories from fat

3 g fat

1 g saturated fat

42 g protein

12 g carbohydrates

Variations:

- Substitute Italian seasoning for the herbes de Provence and add ¼ cup freshly grated Parmesan cheese to the crumb mixture.
- Add 2 tablespoons Dijon mustard to the yogurt mixture; substitute Cajun seasoning for the herbes de Provence, salt, and pepper.
- Substitute corn flakes for the rice cereal.

Long before there were commercial coatings like "Shake 'n Bake" on the market, cooks realized that baking chicken in a coating in the oven replicated the crispy texture of fried chicken. You can use the same approach to thin slices of pork loin, too.

Italian Chicken and Mushrooms

This dish is a version of chicken cacciatore. It's subtly seasoned, and sauces the chicken with tomatoes and lots of herbs. Serve the sauce over some whole-wheat pasta or brown rice.

Yield: 6 servings | **Active time:** 20 minutes | **Start to finish:** 55 minutes

6 (6-ounce) skinless chicken breasts, with bones
2 tablespoons olive oil
1 medium onion, peeled and diced
3 garlic cloves, peeled and minced
1 green bell pepper, seeds and ribs removed, and diced
$^3/_4$ pound mushrooms, wiped with a damp paper towel, trimmed, and sliced
$^1/_2$ cup dry white wine
1 (14.5-ounce) can diced tomatoes, undrained
1 (8-ounce) can tomato sauce
2 tablespoons chopped fresh parsley
1 tablespoon Italian seasoning
Salt and freshly ground black pepper to taste

1. Preheat the oven broiler, and line a broiler pan with heavy-duty aluminum foil. Rinse chicken and pat dry with paper towels. Broil chicken pieces for 3–5 minutes or until browned. Turn pieces, and brown the other side. Transfer chicken to a roasting pan, bone side up, and preheat the oven to 375°F.
2. While chicken browns, heat oil in a large skillet over medium-high heat, swirling to coat the pan. Add onion, garlic, green bell pepper, and mushrooms. Cook, stirring frequently, for 5–7 minutes, or until mushrooms soften. Add wine, tomatoes, tomato sauce, parsley, and Italian seasoning. Bring to a boil over medium-high heat, stirring occasionally.
3. Pour sauce over chicken in the roasting pan. Bake chicken, covered, for 30–40 minutes, or until chicken is cooked through and no longer pink, and an instant-read thermometer registers 170°F.
4. Remove chicken from the pan with tongs, and keep warm. Place the roasting pan on the stove and reduce sauce by $^1/_4$ over high heat, stirring frequently. Season to taste with salt and pepper, and serve immediately.

Note: The chicken can be cooked up to 2 days in advance and refrigerated, tightly covered. Reheat it, covered, in a 350°F oven for 20–25 minutes, or until hot.

Each serving contains:
267 calories
53 calories from fat
6 g fat
1 g saturated fat
41 g protein
9 g carbohydrates

Variation:
- Substitute thick white-fleshed fish fillets for the chicken. They do not need to be browned, and should be added to the sauce and baked for 10–15 minutes, or until cooked through and the fish flakes easily.

Not only is chicken on the bone a lower cost than boneless breasts, the bones actually keep more moisture in the meat when a dish is being baked.

Chicken and Vegetable Fajitas

Fajitas are authentically Mexican, and because the meat and vegetables are grilled, they are loaded with flavor for few calories. To make them even leaner, serve the filling in lettuce leaves rather than tortillas.

Yield: 6 servings | **Active time:** 25 minutes | **Start to finish:** 45 minutes, including 30 minutes for marinating

1¼ pounds boneless, skinless chicken breast halves
1 cup chopped fresh cilantro
¼ cup lime juice
¼ cup orange juice
2 garlic cloves, peeled and minced
1 tablespoon ground cumin
1 tablespoon chili powder
Salt and freshly ground black pepper to taste
¼ cup olive oil
2 green bell peppers, seeds and ribs removed, and quartered
2 sweet onions, such as Vidalia or Bermuda, peeled and cut into
   ½-inch slices
6 (8-inch) whole-wheat tortillas
Toppings: salsa, guacamole, plain nonfat yogurt (optional)

1. Light a charcoal or gas grill, or preheat the oven broiler.
2. Trim chicken breasts of all visible fat, and pound to an even thickness of ½ inch between two sheets of plastic wrap. Combine cilantro, lime juice, orange juice, garlic, cumin, chili powder, salt, and pepper in a heavy resealable plastic bag; mix well. Add olive oil, and mix well again. Pour off ¼ cup, and set aside. Add chicken breasts to remaining marinade, and turn well to coat evenly. Marinate chicken for 30 minutes at room temperature, turning the bag occasionally.
3. While chicken marinates, grill peppers and onions for a total of 10–12 minutes, or until tender, turning once. Remove vegetables from the grill, and when cool enough to handle, cut into thin strips.
4. Remove chicken from marinade, and discard marinade. Grill chicken for 2–3 minutes per side, uncovered, or until chicken is cooked through and no longer pink. Grill tortillas for 30 seconds per side, or soften them in a microwave oven, wrapped in plastic wrap, for 20 seconds.

5. To serve, cut chicken crosswise into thin strips, and add to vegetable mixture. Drizzle mixture with remaining marinade. Place a portion of mixture on the bottom edge of 1 tortilla. Fold over one side, and roll tortilla firmly but gently to enclose filling. Serve immediately, passing salsa, guacamole, or yogurt separately, if using.

Note: Marinade can be made up to 2 days in advance and refrigerated, tightly covered.

Each serving contains:
351 calories
84 calories from fat
9 g fat
1 g saturated fat
28 g protein
38 g carbohydrates

Variation:
- For beef fajitas, substitute flank steak or skirt steak for the chicken. Marinate the beef for 2–3 hours, refrigerated. Grill or broil for 3–5 minutes per side, or to desired doneness.
- For vegetarian fajitas, substitute slices of zucchini or yellow squash for the chicken. It cooks in the same amount of time.

Chicken Marsala

Now here's a healthy dish that's on the table in less time than it takes to get that pizza delivered! The sauce is lean, but contains lots of garlic as well as heady Marsala wine; serve the sauce over some whole-wheat pasta or brown rice.

Yield: 6 servings | **Active time:** 15 minutes | **Start to finish:** 25 minutes

1¼ pounds boneless, skinless chicken breast halves

3 tablespoons all-purpose flour

Salt and freshly ground black pepper to taste

2 tablespoons olive oil

1 small onion, peeled and diced

6 garlic cloves, peeled and minced

1 pound white mushrooms, wiped with a damp paper towel, stemmed, and thinly sliced

³/₄ cup dry Marsala wine

³/₄ cup Chicken Stock (recipe on page 40) or purchased stock

¹/₄ cup chopped fresh parsley

2 teaspoons dried sage

1. Rinse chicken and pat dry with paper towels. Trim chicken of all visible fat, and cut into 1-inch cubes. Season flour to taste with salt and pepper. Dust chicken with seasoned flour, shaking off any excess.

2. Heat olive oil in a heavy, large skillet over medium-high heat, swirling to coat the pan. Add chicken pieces, and cook, stirring frequently, for 3 minutes, or until chicken is opaque. Remove chicken from the pan with a slotted spoon, and set aside.

3. Add onion, garlic, and mushrooms to the skillet. Cook, stirring frequently, for 3 minutes, or until onion is translucent. Return chicken to the skillet, and add Marsala, stock, parsley, and sage. Bring to a boil, stirring occasionally.

4. Reduce the heat to medium, and simmer mixture, uncovered, for 10–15 minutes, or until chicken is cooked through and no longer pink. Season to taste with salt and pepper. Serve immediately.

Note: The dish can be prepared up to 1 day in advance and refrigerated, tightly covered. Reheat it over low heat, covered, until hot.

Each serving contains:
197 calories
52 calories from fat
6 g fat
1 g saturated fat
25.5 g protein
11 g carbohydrates

Variation:
- Substitute boneless pork loin, cut into thin strips, for the chicken.

If you're using canned or boxed stock for a dish, and have some left in the container, don't waste it; make ice cubes from it. Measure the capacity of your ice cube tray with a measuring tablespoon, and once the cubes are frozen, transfer them to a resealable plastic bag. If you need a few tablespoons of stock you're all set.

Turkey Stew with Marsala and Sage

While cooking with heady Marsala is a part of Italian cuisine, adding fresh sage to this hearty, comforting strew is also reminiscent of the flavors of traditional American poultry stuffing.

Yield: 6 servings | **Active time:** 20 minutes | **Start to finish:** 55 minutes

1 tablespoon unsalted butter

1½ pounds turkey breast meat, cut into 1-inch cubes

¾ pound mushrooms, wiped with a damp paper towel, trimmed, and quartered

2 medium onions, peeled and diced

1 garlic clove, peeled and minced

1½ cups Chicken Stock (recipe on page 40) or purchased stock

⅓ cup dry Marsala wine

3 tablespoons chopped fresh parsley

1 teaspoon dried sage

1½ teaspoons cornstarch

2 tablespoons cold water

Salt and freshly ground black pepper to taste

1. Melt butter in a large, deep skillet over medium-high heat, swirling to coat the pan. Add turkey, and brown on all sides. Remove turkey from the pan with a slotted spoon and set aside. Add mushrooms, onions, and garlic, and cook, stirring frequently, for 5–7 minutes, or until mushrooms soften.

2. Add stock, Marsala, parsley, and sage, and bring to a boil over high heat. Reduce the heat to medium, and simmer mixture, stirring frequently, until reduced by ½. Return turkey to the pan, and cook over low heat, uncovered, for 20 minutes, stirring occasionally.

3. Mix cornstarch with water in a small cup. Stir into the pan, and cook for 2 minutes, or until slightly thickened. Season to taste with salt and pepper, and serve immediately.

Note: The stew can be made up to 2 days in advance, and refrigerated, tightly covered. Reheat it, covered, over low heat, stirring occasionally.

Each serving contains:

172 calories

33 calories from fat

4 g fat
2 g saturated fat
28 g protein
7 g carbohydrates

Variation:

• Substitute 1 pound boneless pork loin for the turkey.

It's important in recipes to cook the mushrooms as long as directed. While they would eventually soften while simmering in the sauce, by pre-cooking them much of the innate liquid content evaporates so it doesn't dilute the sauce.

Sweet and Spicy Chinese Chicken

The pitfall to enjoying stir-fried dishes in Chinese restaurants is the amount of oil used in their preparation. This fiery dish, ready in mere minutes, uses very little oil but has lots of varied seasonings and contains a good serving of vegetables. Serve it with brown rice.

Yield: 6 servings | **Active time:** 25 minutes | **Start to finish:** 25 minutes

    1 pound boneless, skinless chicken breast halves
    2 tablespoons cornstarch
    2 tablespoons dry sherry
    2 tablespoons reduced-sodium soy sauce
    1 tablespoon rice vinegar
    6 scallions
    1 cup Chicken Stock (recipe on page 40) or purchased stock
    ⅓ cup plum sauce *
    1 teaspoon Chinese five-spice powder *
    2 tablespoons vegetable oil
    4 garlic cloves, peeled and minced
    2 tablespoons grated fresh ginger
    1 celery rib, rinsed, trimmed, and thinly sliced on the diagonal
    1 medium carrot, peeled and thinly sliced on the diagonal
    1 green bell pepper, seeds and ribs removed, and thinly sliced
    Salt and freshly ground black pepper to taste

1. Rinse chicken and pat dry with paper towels. Trim chicken of all visible fat. Cut chicken into ½-inch cubes. Place chicken in a mixing bowl, and sprinkle with cornstarch. Toss to coat evenly, and add sherry, soy sauce and vinegar, tossing again to coat evenly. Set aside.

2. Rinse and trim scallions. Cut scallions into 1-inch lengths and then slice lengthwise into thin strips. Set aside. Combine stock, plum sauce, and five-spice powder in a small bowl. Stir well, and set aside.

3. Heat vegetable oil in a heavy wok or large skillet over high heat, swirling to coat the pan. Add scallions, garlic, and ginger, and stir-fry for 30 seconds, or until fragrant, stirring constantly. Add chicken and cook for 1 minute, stirring constantly. Add celery, carrot, and green bell pepper, and stir-fry vegetables for 2 minutes more, stirring constantly.

* Available in the Asian aisle of most supermarkets and in specialty markets.

4. Add sauce mixture and cook, stirring constantly, for 2 minutes, or until chicken is cooked through and no longer pink and sauce is slightly thickened. Season to taste with salt and pepper, and serve immediately.

Note: The chicken, vegetables, and sauce can be prepped up to 6 hours in advance and refrigerated, tightly covered.

Each serving contains:
199 calories
50 calories from fat
6 g fat
1 g saturated fat
20 g protein
15 g carbohydrates

Variations:
- For a spicy dish, add 1 jalapeño or serrano chile, seeds and ribs removed, and finely chopped, to the pan along with the scallions, garlic, and ginger.
- Substitute Asian sesame oil for the vegetable oil, and sprinkle the cooked dish with 2 tablespoons toasted sesame seeds.
- Substitute boneless pork loin for the chicken.

Chinese five-spice powder is perhaps the oldest blend of spices around. Having been used in traditional Chinese cooking for centuries, it's made up of equal parts cinnamon, cloves, fennel seed, star anise, and Szechwan peppercorns. It's available in most supermarkets, found either with spices or with Asian food.

Stir-Fried Ginger Chicken with Broccoli

Broccoli is touted as being one of the super-foods that helps keep your immune system in good working order. It's also delicious when flavored with the Asian seasonings in this dish. Serve it with some brown rice, and your meal is complete.

Yield: 6 servings | **Active time:** 25 minutes | **Start to finish:** 25 minutes

1 pound boneless, skinless chicken breast halves
⅓ cup reduced-sodium soy sauce, divided
¼ cup honey, divided
5 garlic cloves, peeled and minced, divided
½ teaspoon crushed red pepper flakes, or to taste, divided
¾ cup Chicken Stock (recipe on page 40) or purchased stock
1 tablespoon cornstarch
1 tablespoon cold water
2 tablespoons vegetable oil
4 scallions, white parts and 4 inches of green tops, rinsed, trimmed, and thinly sliced
3 tablespoons grated fresh ginger
½ pound fresh broccoli, rinsed and cut into florets, with stems peeled and sliced
Salt and freshly ground black pepper to taste

1. Rinse chicken and pat dry with paper towels. Trim chicken of all visible fat. Cut chicken into ½-inch cubes. Combine 2 tablespoons soy sauce, 2 tablespoons honey, 2 garlic cloves, and ¼ teaspoon red pepper flakes in a mixing bowl. Stir well, add chicken, and mix well. Set aside. Combine remaining soy sauce, honey, red pepper flakes, and chicken stock in a small bowl, and set aside. Combine cornstarch with water in a small bowl, stir well, and set aside.

2. Heat vegetable oil in a heavy wok or skillet over high heat, swirling to coat the pan. Add scallions, remaining garlic, and ginger, and stir-fry for 30 seconds, or until fragrant. Add chicken and cook for 2 minutes, stirring constantly. Add broccoli, and stir-fry for 2 minutes more, stirring constantly.

3. Add sauce mixture and cook, stirring constantly, for 2 minutes, or until chicken is cooked through and no longer pink. Add cornstarch

* Available in the Asian aisle of most supermarkets and in specialty markets.

mixture and simmer for 1 minute, or until slightly thickened. Season to taste with salt and pepper, and serve immediately.

Note: The chicken, vegetables, and sauce can be prepped up to 6 hours in advance and refrigerated, tightly covered.

Each serving contains:
217 calories
50 calories from fat
5.5 g fat
1 g saturated fat
21 g protein
21.5 g carbohydrates

Variations:
- Substitute asparagus, woody stems discarded and cut into 1-inch lengths, for the broccoli.
- Substitute fresh green beans, trimmed and cut into 1-inch lengths, for the broccoli.
- Substitute boneless pork loin for the chicken.

Remember that part of being a savvy cook is not being wasteful, and broccoli crowns—which are just the florets—are much more expensive than using the whole stalks. Do peel the stems, because the peel is tough and woody, but use a whole stalk.

Spicy Chinese Chicken Kebabs

Thread some chicken onto skewers, fire up the "barbie," and you're ready to enjoy a treat! The sauce is easy to make, and it's also versatile as a dipping sauce for Asian hors d'oeuvres. Add some stir-fried vegetables or vegetable lo mein to your plate and dinner is complete.

Yield: 6 servings | **Active time:** 15 minutes | **Start to finish:** 45 minutes

    12 bamboo skewers
    1½ pounds boneless, skinless chicken thighs
    ⅓ cup unsweetened applesauce
    ¼ cup hoisin sauce *
    2 tablespoons firmly packed dark brown sugar
    3 tablespoons ketchup
    1 tablespoon honey
    1 tablespoon rice vinegar
    1 tablespoon reduced-sodium soy sauce
    2 teaspoons Chinese chile paste with garlic *, or to taste (or substitute hot red pepper sauce)

1. Light a charcoal or gas grill, or preheat the oven broiler. Soak bamboo skewers in water to cover for 30 minutes.
2. Rinse chicken and pat dry with paper towels. Trim chicken of all visible fat. Cut chicken into strips 2 inches long and ½ inch wide.
3. Combine applesauce, hoisin sauce, brown sugar, ketchup, honey, vinegar, soy sauce, and Chinese chile paste in a mixing bowl. Whisk until smooth, and divide sauce into 2 small bowls.
4. Thread chicken onto skewers and place over a hot fire. Grill chicken, basting with sauce every 2 minutes, for 3–5 minutes per side. Discard basting sauce. Remove chicken from the grill, and serve immediately, passing second bowl of sauce separately.

Note: The sauce can be prepared up to 3 days in advance and refrigerated, tightly covered. Also, the chicken can be cooked up to 1 day in advance and served at room temperature or chilled.

* Available in the Asian aisle of most supermarkets and in specialty markets.

Each serving contains:

167 calories

42 calories from fat

5 g fat

1 g saturated fat

24 g protein

8 g carbohydrates

Variations:
- Substitute strips of boneless pork loin for the chicken.
- Add small cubes of zucchini or small mushrooms to the skewers with the chicken.

To save time when making a recipe with many liquid ingredients, measure them into the same large cup, calculating what the level should be after each addition.

Sesame Chicken and Zucchini Kebabs

These succulent morsels of chicken alternating with delicate squash are wonderful for a buffet dinner because they don't require a knife to cut them. The Asian marinade imparts wonderful flavor quickly, and all you need is some steamed brown rice to complete the meal.

Yield: 6 servings | **Active time:** 15 minutes | **Start to finish:** 1 hour, including 30 minutes for marinating

> 6 (8-inch) bamboo skewers
> 6 boneless, skinless chicken thighs
> 2 small zucchini
> 3 garlic cloves, peeled and minced
> 4 scallions, white parts and 2 inches of green tops, rinsed, trimmed and chopped
> $1/2$ cup reduced-sodium soy sauce
> $1/2$ cup dry sherry
> Freshly ground black pepper to taste
> 2 tablespoons Asian sesame oil *
> $1/2$ teaspoon Chinese chile oil *
> $1/4$ cup sesame seeds *

1. Soak bamboo skewers in water to cover for 30 minutes. Rinse chicken and pat dry with paper towels. Cut chicken into 1-inch cubes, and set aside. Cut zucchini into 1-inch cubes, and set aside.
2. Combine garlic, scallions, soy sauce, sherry, and pepper in a heavy resealable plastic bag, and mix well. Add sesame oil and chile oil, and mix well again. Add chicken and zucchini cubes to the bag, and marinate at room temperature for 30 minutes, turning the bag occasionally.
3. Light a charcoal or gas grill, or preheat the oven broiler. Remove chicken and zucchini from marinade, discard marinade, and thread chicken and zucchini onto skewers. Place sesame seeds on a sheet of plastic wrap, and press skewers into sesame seeds.
4. Grill or broil skewers for 5–7 minutes per side, or until chicken is cooked through and no longer pink. Serve immediately.

Note: The chicken can be marinated for up to 4 hours, refrigerated.

* Available in the Asian aisle of most supermarkets and in specialty markets.

Each serving contains:
137 calories
56 calories from fat
6 g fat
1 g saturated fat
16 g protein
4 g carbohydrates

Variations:
- Substitute cubes of pork loin or sirloin tip for the chicken.
- Substitute cubes of eggplant or small mushrooms for the zuc-chini.

Foods such as sesame seeds are very expensive if purchased in the spice section of supermarkets but extremely inexpensive at Asian groceries. The same is true of spices like curry powder and tumeric; buy them at Indian groceries rather than at the supermarket.

Chicken Thighs with Yogurt Mint Sauce

While many Americans think of mint in the context of heady juleps or a sweet jelly to serve with lamb, in both Middle Eastern and Indian cooking it is a versatile culinary herb. These thighs are marinated in a yogurt base that tenderizes them, and then topped with a minty-fresh sauce.

Yield: 6 servings | **Active time:** 20 minutes | **Start to finish:** 3³/₄ hours, including 3 hours for marinating

12 boneless, skinless chicken thighs

1¹/₂ cups plain nonfat yogurt, divided

¹/₂ cup lemon juice

3 garlic cloves, peeled and minced, divided

1 tablespoon ground coriander

1 teaspoon dried thyme

Salt and freshly ground black pepper to taste

2 tablespoons chopped fresh parsley

1 tablespoon chopped fresh mint

1 tablespoon olive oil

1 small red onion, peeled and thinly sliced

1 large tomato, rinsed, cored, seeded, and chopped

1. Rinse chicken and pat dry with paper towels. Prick chicken all over with a meat fork.
2. Combine 1 cup yogurt, lemon juice, 2 garlic cloves, coriander, thyme, salt, and pepper in a heavy resealable plastic bag. Mix well. Add chicken and marinate, refrigerated, for at least 3 hours or up to 24 hours, turning the bag occasionally.
3. While chicken marinates, prepare sauce. Combine remaining ¹/₂ cup yogurt, remaining garlic clove, parsley, mint, salt, and pepper in a mixing bowl, and whisk well. Refrigerate sauce until ready to serve, tightly covered.
4. Light a charcoal or gas grill, or preheat the oven broiler.
5. Heat olive oil in a small skillet over medium-high heat. Add onion and cook, stirring frequently, for 3–5 minutes, or until onion is translucent. Add tomato, and cook for 3 minutes, stirring occasionally. Season mixture to taste with salt and pepper, and set aside.

6. Remove chicken from marinade, and discard marinade. Cook chicken for 10–12 minutes per side, or until cooked through and no longer pink. To serve, place chicken on each plate and top with some of onion mixture; pass sauce separately.

Note: Both the sauce and the onion mixture can be prepared up to 6 hours in advance. Refrigerate sauce and keep onion mixture at room temperature.

Each serving contains:
208 calories
65 calories from fat
7 g fat
2 g saturated fat
29 g protein
5.5 g carbohydrates

Variation:
- Substitute sirloin tips or flank steak for the chicken. Grill for 3–4 minutes per side, or to desired doneness.

Spanish Chicken Salad

Many dishes in traditional Spanish cooking include succulent fresh oranges, so a salad such as this one is a good way to add some fruit servings to your day. The smoked paprika gives the chicken a grilled flavor, even though it's sautéed on the stove.

Yield: 6 servings | **Active time:** 20 minutes | **Start to finish:** 50 minutes, including 30 minutes for marinating

> 1¼ pounds boneless, skinless chicken breast halves
> ¾ cup orange juice
> 1 small onion, peeled and diced
> 3 garlic cloves, peeled and minced
> 2 tablespoons smoked Spanish paprika
> Salt and freshly ground black pepper to taste
> 2 tablespoons olive oil, divided
> 6 cups bite-sized pieces iceberg lettuce or romaine, rinsed and dried
> 2 navel oranges, peeled and sliced
> 2 small fennel bulbs, stem trimmed, stalks discarded, cored, and thinly sliced

1. Rinse chicken and pat dry with paper towels. Trim all visible fat from chicken and cut it into thin slices against the grain. Combine orange juice, onion, garlic, paprika, salt, and pepper in a jar with a tight-fitting lid. Shake well. Add 1 tablespoon oil, and shake well again. Pour ½ of dressing into a heavy resealable plastic bag. Add chicken, and marinate at room temperature for 30 minutes, turning the bag occasionally.

2. Place lettuce on a serving platter or individual plates, and arrange orange and fennel slices on top.

3. Heat remaining oil in a large skillet over medium-high heat, swirling to coat the pan. Drain chicken from marinade, and pat dry on paper towels. Discard marinade. Cook chicken, stirring constantly, for 3 minutes, or until chicken is cooked through and no longer pink. Place chicken on top of salad, drizzle salad with remaining dressing, and serve immediately.

Note: The chicken can marinate for up to 4 hours refrigerated, and the remaining dressing can be made at that time and kept at room temperature.

Each serving contains:
202 calories
41 calories from fat
4.5 g fat
1 g saturated fat
24 g protein
17 g carbohydrates

Variation:
- Substitute 1 pound boneless pork loin for the chicken.

> While the ribs are trimmed off of fennel bulbs before the bulbs are used, they should certainly not go to waste. Use them in place of celery in salads and soups.

Chicken and Eggplant Cannelloni

Rather than using commercial cannelloni shells, which I find contain too much dough relative to the amount of filling, I started using egg roll wrappers to create stuffed pastas. They cook in the sauce, and the resulting dish is light yet filling.

Yield: 6 servings | **Active time:** 20 minutes | **Start to finish:** 1¾ hours

> 3 (1-pound) eggplants
> 1 tablespoon olive oil
> 1 large onion, peeled and chopped
> 3 garlic cloves, peeled and minced
> 3 cups shredded cooked chicken
> 2 tablespoons freshly grated Parmesan cheese
> Salt and freshly ground black pepper to taste
> 6 egg roll wrappers
> 2 cups Herbed Tomato Sauce (recipe on page 38) or purchased
>   marinara sauce
> ½ cup grated part-skim mozzarella cheese

1. Preheat the oven to 400°F, and line a baking sheet with aluminum foil. Prick the eggplants with a sharp meat fork, and place on the baking sheet. Bake eggplants for 40–50 minutes, turning after 20 minutes, or until they are uniformly soft. Remove eggplants from the oven. They will look brown and will have deflated. When cool enough to handle easily, cut off tops and peel away skin with your fingers. Drain any liquid that develops by shaking pulp in a sieve. Chop flesh either by hand or in a food processor fitted with the steel blade, using on-and-off pulsing. Set aside.

2. While eggplants bake, heat oil in a small skillet over medium heat, swirling to coat the pan. Add onion and garlic, and cook, stirring frequently, for 10 minutes, or until onion is soft.

3. Reduce the oven temperature to 350°F. Combine eggplant, chicken, onion mixture, Parmesan cheese, salt, and pepper in a mixing bowl. Divide mixture evenly and place a portion along the top edge of each egg roll wrapper. Gently roll them into tube shapes and lay them, seam side down, in a 9 x 13-inch baking pan.

4. Pour tomato sauce over top of rolls, cover the pan with foil, and bake for 20 minutes. Remove the foil, sprinkle mozzarella cheese evenly over the top, and return the pan to the oven for 10 minutes. Serve immediately.

Note: The eggplant/chicken mixture and the tomato sauce can be prepared up to 2 days in advance, and the cannelloni can be assembled up to 6 hours in advance. Do not bake it, however, until just prior to serving.

Each serving contains:
357 calories
79 calories from fat
9 g fat
3 g saturated fat
31 g protein
39 g carbohydrates

Variations:
- Substitute cooked fish for the chicken.
- Substitute sautéed zucchini or yellow squash for the chicken.

While eggplants are inherently very healthy and low in calories, the problem arises in how they're frequently cooked—with a lot of fat. That's why baking them, either whole or in slices, is preferable.

Chicken in Lettuce Cups

Leaves of crispy iceberg lettuce make the perfect low-calorie wrapper; you can use them for tacos or other fillings, too. For this traditional and authentic Chinese dish, the low-calorie ground chicken is stir-fried with water chestnuts to give the filling additional crunch.

Yield: 6 servings | **Active time:** 20 minutes | **Start to finish:** 20 minutes

    3 tablespoons reduced-sodium soy sauce
    2 tablespoons hoisin sauce *
    2 tablespoons rice vinegar
    2 teaspoons cornstarch
    1 tablespoon Asian sesame oil *
    3 garlic cloves, peeled and minced
    2 tablespoons grated fresh ginger
    6 scallions, white parts and 4 inches of green tops, rinsed,
       trimmed, and thinly sliced, divided
    1 pound ground chicken
    1 (8-ounce) can water chestnuts, drained, rinsed, and chopped
    Salt and freshly ground black pepper to taste
    12–18 leaves iceberg lettuce, rinsed and dried

1. Mix soy sauce, hoisin sauce, vinegar, and cornstarch in a small bowl. Stir well, and set aside.
2. Heat sesame oil in a large skillet over medium-high heat, swirling to coat the pan. Add garlic, ginger, and ⅔ of scallions. Stir-fry for 30 seconds, stirring constantly, or until fragrant. Add chicken, and stir-fry for 3–4 minutes, breaking up lumps with a fork, or until chicken has lost all of its pink color and is white and beginning to brown. Stir in water chestnuts, and stir-fry 1 minute.
3. Add sauce mixture to the pan, and when mixture boils and thickens, reduce the heat to low and simmer for 1 minute, stirring frequently. Season to taste with salt and pepper.
4. To serve, spoon chicken into lettuce leaves, sprinkling each serving with remaining scallions. Serve immediately.

Note: The chicken mixture can be prepared up to 1 day in advance and refrigerated, tightly covered. Reheat it over low heat or in a micro-wave oven before serving.

* Available in the Asian aisle of most supermarkets and in specialty markets.

Each serving contains:

165 calories
72 calories from fat
8 g fat
2 g saturated fat
14.5 g protein
9 g carbohydrates

Variation:

- Substitute ground pork for the ground chicken.

Hoisin sauce, pronounced *hoy-ZAHN,* is the ketchup of Chinese cooking. This thick, sweet, and spicy reddish-brown sauce is a mixture of soybeans, garlic, chiles, Chinese five-spice powder, and sugar. Like ketchup, it's used both as a condiment and as an ingredient.

Chicken Loaf with Spinach

This is such a pretty dish to serve! There's a "tunnel" of bright green spinach hidden in the middle of a meatloaf made with lean chicken and dotted with bright orange carrot, and it's ready to cook in a matter of minutes.

Yield: 6 servings | **Active time:** 15 minutes | **Start to finish:** 1½ hours

2 teaspoons unsalted butter

1 large onion, peeled and finely chopped

1 garlic clove, peeled and minced

¼ cup grated carrot

1¼ pounds ground chicken

2 tablespoons plain breadcrumbs

1 large egg, lightly beaten

2 large egg whites

2 teaspoons herbes de Provence

Salt and freshly ground black pepper to taste

1 (10-ounce) package frozen chopped spinach, thawed and squeezed dry

¼ cup grated part-skim mozzarella cheese

Vegetable oil spray

1. Preheat the oven to 350°F, and grease a 9 x 5-inch loaf pan with vegetable oil spray.
2. Heat butter in a small skillet over medium-high heat. Add onion, garlic, and carrot, and cook, stirring frequently, for 3 minutes, or until onion is translucent. Scrape mixture into a large mixing bowl, and allow to cool for 5 minutes.
3. Add chicken, breadcrumbs, egg, egg whites, herbes de Provence, salt, and pepper to the mixing bowl, and mix well. Combine spinach and cheese in another mixing bowl, and season to taste with salt and pepper.
4. Place ½ of chicken in the lightly oiled loaf pan, and make a tunnel, placing spinach mixture in the center. Top with remaining chicken, and smooth the top with a spatula.
5. Bake for 1 hour, or until an instant-read thermometer registers 175°F. Remove meatloaf from the oven, and allow to rest for 10 minutes. Serve immediately.

Note: The dish can be prepared up to 2 days in advance and refrigerated, tightly covered. Reheat it, covered, in a 350°F oven for 20–25 minutes, or until hot.

Each serving contains:
211 calories
100 calories from fat
11 g fat
4 g saturated fat
22 g protein
7 g carbohydrates

Variations:
- Substitute ground pork for the ground chicken.
- Substitute frozen chopped broccoli, cooked according to package directions, for the spinach.

The reason why frozen spinach needs no precooking is that the blanching it receives truly cooks it. It is important, however, to squeeze it dry before using it or the inherent water will make a dish "soupy."

Tandoori Chicken

This healthful Indian dish is briefly marinated in seasoned yogurt, which tenderizes the chicken as well as flavoring it.

Yield: 6 servings | **Active time:** 15 minutes | **Start to finish:** 45 minutes, including 30 minutes for marinating

    1¼ pounds boneless, skinless chicken breast halves
    ¾ cup plain nonfat yogurt
    2 tablespoons lemon juice
    3 garlic cloves, peeled and pressed through a garlic press
    1 tablespoon grated fresh ginger
    1 tablespoon ground turmeric
    2 teaspoons ground coriander
    1 teaspoon ground cumin
    Salt and cayenne to taste
    Vegetable oil spray

1. Light a charcoal or gas grill, or preheat the oven broiler.
2. Trim chicken breasts of all visible fat, and pound to an even thickness of ½ inch between two sheets of plastic wrap. Combine yogurt, lemon juice, garlic, ginger, turmeric, coriander, cumin, salt, and cayenne in a heavy resealable plastic bag. Add chicken, and marinate at room temperature for 30 minutes, turning the bag occasionally.
3. Remove chicken from marinade, and discard marinade. Pat chicken dry with paper towels, and spray with vegetable oil. Grill chicken for 2–3 minutes per side, uncovered, or until chicken is cooked through and no longer pink. Cut chicken into slices, and serve immediately.

Note: The marinade can be prepared up to 1 day in advance and refrigerated, tightly covered.

Each serving contains:
120 calories
12 calories from fat
1 g fat
0 g saturated fat
23 g protein
3 g carbohydrates

Variation:
- Substitute thin white-fleshed fish fillets for the chicken. They will cook in the same amount of time.

Southwestern Turkey Sausage with Yogurt Dill Dressing

The spiciness of this sausage, with its decidedly Southwestern accent, is cooled by the creamy, light dressing. The dish can also be made into miniatures and skewered on toothpicks for cocktail parties.

Yield: 6 servings | **Active time:** 15 minutes | **Start to finish:** 20 minutes

> 4 teaspoons olive oil, divided
> 1 large onion, peeled and finely chopped
> 2 garlic cloves, peeled and minced
> 2 celery ribs, rinsed, trimmed, and finely chopped
> 1 large jalapeño or serrano chile, seeds and ribs removed, and finely chopped
> 1 pound ground turkey
> 1/3 cup crushed tortilla chips
> 1 tablespoon white wine vinegar
> 1/2 cup chopped fresh cilantro
> 2 teaspoons ground cumin
> Salt and freshly ground black pepper to taste
> 1/2 cup Yogurt Dill Dressing (recipe on page 31)

1. Light a charcoal or gas grill, or preheat the oven broiler.
2. Heat 2 teaspoons oil in a medium skillet over medium heat. Add onion, garlic, celery, and chile, and cook, stirring frequently, for 7–10 minutes, or until vegetables are soft.
3. Scrape mixture into a mixing bowl, and add turkey, crushed tortilla chips, vinegar, cilantro, cumin, salt, and pepper. Form turkey mixture into 12 patties, about 1/2 inch thick, and brush with remaining oil.
4. Grill or broil patties for 3–4 minutes per side, or until cooked through and no longer pink. Serve immediately, passing dressing separately.

Note: The sausage mixture can be made 1 day in advance and refrigerated, tightly covered. Grill or broil the patties just prior to serving.

Each serving contains:
174 calories
79 calories from fat
9 g fat
2 g saturated fat
15 g protein
8 g carbohydrates

Herbed Turkey Sausage

These sausages are savory and redolent of herbs without being spicy. You can make the mixture into sausage balls and serve them with more tomato sauce on top of pasta, or use them as an hors d'oeuvre; you can also serve them (minus the sauce, perhaps) at breakfast in place of high-calorie foods like bacon.

Yield: 6 servings | **Active time:** 20 minutes | **Start to finish:** 30 minutes

4 teaspoons olive oil, divided
1 large onion, peeled and finely chopped
3 garlic cloves, peeled and minced
2 celery ribs, rinsed, trimmed, and finely chopped
1 small carrot, peeled and grated
1 pound ground turkey
$1/3$ cup Italian breadcrumbs
1 large egg white, lightly beaten
2 teaspoons dried sage
1 teaspoon dried oregano
1 teaspoon dried basil
$1/2$ teaspoon dried thyme
Salt and freshly ground black pepper to taste
$3/4$ cup Herbed Tomato Sauce (recipe on page 38) or purchased marinara sauce, heated

1. Light a charcoal or gas grill, or preheat the oven broiler.
2. Heat 2 teaspoons oil in a medium skillet over medium heat. Add onion, garlic, celery, and carrot. Cook, stirring frequently, for 7–10 minutes, or until vegetables are soft.
3. Scrape mixture into a mixing bowl, and add turkey, breadcrumbs, egg white, sage, oregano, basil, thyme, salt, and pepper. Form turkey mixture into 12 sausage-shaped cylinders, and brush with remaining oil.
4. Grill or broil for a total of 8 minutes, turning a quarter turn every 2 minutes, or until sausages are cooked through and no longer pink. To serve, place 2 tablespoons of the tomato sauce on each plate and top with 2 sausages.

Note: The sausage mixture can be made 1 day in advance and refrigerated, tightly covered. Grill or broil the sausages just prior to serving.

Each serving contains:
200 calories
94 calories from fat
10 g fat
2 g saturated fat
15 g protein
11 g carbohydrates

Variation:
- Substitute ground pork for the ground turkey.

Ingredients in all recipes serve a function. In traditional sausage recipes, it's the fat that gives the dish moisture. When doing low-calorie cooking, the same moisture is provided by the high percentage of vegetables.

Turkey Picadillo

Picadillo, which means "small bits and pieces," is a popular Mexican meat stew made with a variety of meats. It has a slight sweet and sour flavor from the addition of olives and raisins, but falls clearly into the family of chili con carne. Serve it with some brown rice and a tossed salad.

Yield: 6 servings | **Active time:** 15 minutes | **Start to finish:** 40 minutes

    1 tablespoon olive oil
    1 pound ground turkey
    1 large onion, peeled and diced
    3 garlic cloves, peeled and minced
    2 tablespoons chili powder
    1 teaspoon dried oregano
    1 teaspoon ground cumin
    $^3/_4$ teaspoon ground cinnamon
    $^1/_4$–$^1/_2$ teaspoon crushed red pepper flakes
    $^1/_4$ cup raisins
    $^1/_4$ cup chopped green olives
    1 (14.5-ounce) can diced tomatoes, undrained
    1 (8-ounce) can tomato sauce
    1 (15-ounce) can pinto beans, drained and rinsed
    Salt and freshly ground black pepper to taste

1. Heat oil in a saucepan over medium-high heat, swirling to coat the pan. Add turkey and cook, breaking up lumps with a fork, for 3–5 minutes, or until turkey loses its pink color. Add onion and garlic and cook, stirring frequently, for 3 minutes, or until onion is translucent. Add chili powder, oregano, cumin, cinnamon, and red pepper flakes, and cook for 1 minute, stirring constantly.

2. Add raisins, olives, tomatoes, tomato sauce, and beans to the pan, and stir well. Bring to a boil, then reduce the heat to low, and simmer mixture, partially covered, for 25 minutes, stirring occasionally. Season to taste with salt and pepper, and serve immediately.

Note: The dish can be prepared up to 2 days in advance and refrigerated, tightly covered. Reheat it, covered, over low heat, stirring occasionally.

Each serving contains:

249 calories

94 calories from fat

10.5 g fat

2 g saturated fat

18 g protein

22 g carbohydrates

Variation:

- Substitute ¾ pound ground pork for the turkey.

Any chili or variation on a chili can be turned into finger food by creating nachos. Layer the meat filling on top of some low-fat corn chips, and top the meat with low-fat cheese. Broil the nachos until the cheese melts.

Turkey Chili

This is my favorite way to enjoy chili; there are some "secret ingredients" in the sauce—like cocoa powder and coffee—that really enliven the taste. Serve it over brown rice, and pass bowls of reduced-fat grated cheddar and plain nonfat yogurt separately.

Yield: 6 servings | **Active time:** 15 minutes | **Start to finish:** 45 minutes

1 tablespoon olive oil
1 large onion, peeled and chopped
3 garlic cloves, peeled and minced
1 large green bell pepper, seeds and ribs removed, and chopped
1 jalapeño or serrano chile, seeds and ribs removed, and finely chopped
1¼ pounds ground turkey
2 tablespoons all-purpose flour
3 tablespoons chili powder
2 tablespoons ground cumin
1 tablespoon unsweetened cocoa powder
2 tablespoons cider vinegar
2 tablespoons strong brewed coffee
1 (28-ounce) can crushed tomatoes in tomato puree
1 (15-ounce) can red kidney beans, drained and rinsed
Salt and freshly ground black pepper to taste

1. Heat oil in a Dutch oven over medium-high heat, swirling to coat the pan. Add onion, garlic, green bell pepper, and chile. Cook, stirring frequently, for 3 minutes, or until onion is translucent. Add turkey and cook for 5 minutes, stirring frequently, and breaking up any lumps with a spoon. Stir in flour, chili powder, cumin, and cocoa, and cook, stirring constantly, for 1 minute.

2. Add vinegar, coffee, tomatoes, and kidney beans, and bring to a boil over medium-high heat. Reduce the heat to low, and simmer chili, partially covered, for 40–45 minutes, or until thickened. Season to taste with salt and pepper, and serve immediately.

Note: The dish can be prepared up to 2 days in advance and refrigerated, tightly covered. Reheat it, covered, over low heat until hot, stirring occasionally.

Each serving contains:
289 calories
96 calories from fat
11 g fat
3 g saturated fat
23 g protein
26 g carbohydrates

Variations:
- Substitute 1 pound extra-lean ground beef for the turkey.
- Substitute 1½ pounds zucchini, cut into ½-inch cubes, for the turkey.

Chapter 6:

One If By Land . . . Part 2: Pork and Beef Entrees

Were you fearful that the chapter on meat dishes would be tiny in a low-calorie cookbook? Well, fear not. I'm a devout carnivore, and still eat red meat at least a few times a week. So here's your chapter of hearty dishes that will stick to your ribs, but *not* stick to your waistline.

What you won't find in this chapter are recipes for big hunks of meat. That slab of standing rib roast falling off the sides of your plate is a once a year treat for a holiday—determined by both your budget and your diet. But enjoy it from time to time, as well as a steak coming off the grill in the summer.

What makes these dishes low-calorie is that the quantity of meat is balanced by ingredients that are lower in calories and lower in fat. In some recipes it's beans; in other recipes it's a vegetable or a combination of many vegetables. This is the way that meats are consumed in almost every culture around the world except ours.

Due to both price and calories, there are more recipes for pork in this chapter than there are recipes for beef. If you want to enjoy the delicate taste of ground veal—and can find it on sale—substitute it for the ground pork in any of these recipes. The same is true for generally substituting ground lamb for ground beef if you like the richer flavor of that red meat.

PORCINE PLEASURES

Pork truly is "the other white meat," and is becoming more popular yearly because of its inherent and increasing leanness. Recent studies of randomly selected pork cuts from leading supermarkets in fifteen U.S. cities have shown that today's pork is 31 percent lower in fat, 17 percent lower in calories, and 10 percent lower in cholesterol than it was a few decades ago. In addition, more than 60 percent of the fat in pork is unsaturated. This compares favorably with beef and lamb, which are 52 percent and 44 percent unsaturated, respectively.

Agricultural professionals attribute the reduction of fat content in part to improvements in the breeding and feeding of pigs. Retailers are also trimming fat more closely from pork cuts, so people are getting more lean meat for their dollar.

CREATIVE CUTTING

Remember one of our tenets of low-cost cooking: the more processed a food, the more expensive it will be. For example, boneless pork chops at my supermarket recently were $4.99 pound. Compare that with a boneless pork loin—the same exact piece of meat before it was cut into slices—for $3.79 a pound, and a pork loin with bones for $1.99 per pound. Even if you're not willing to take the time to cut the meat off the bones, it took merely 35 seconds for me to save $2 by cutting the boneless roast into chops.

Compared to the precision needed to cut a whole chicken into its component parts, boning and cutting meat for the recipes in this chapter is a free-for-all. The bones should be removed, however. But do save any beef bones for making Beef Stock (recipe on page 41); unfortunately, pork bones do not make a good stock.

The first step of boning is to cut away the bones. Then cut away any large areas of fat that can be easily discarded. The last step is to decide how the remaining boneless meat should be cut. The rule is to cut across the grain rather than with the grain. If you're not sure which way the grain runs, make a test slice. You should see the ends of fibers if you cut across the grain. The reason for this is that meat becomes more tender if the ends of the fibers are exposed to the liquid and heat.

PROCEDURAL PROWESS

The one major principle for almost all meat dishes is the initial browning of the meat, which means cooking the meat quickly over moderately high heat. This causes the surface of the food to brown. In the case of cubes of beef for stew, browning seals in the juices and keeps the interior moist; for ground meats, browning gives food an appetizing color, allows you to drain off some of the inherent saturated fat, and also gives dishes a rich flavor.

While larger pieces can be browned under an oven broiler, ground meats should be browned in a skillet. Crumble the meat in a skillet over medium-high heat. Break up the lumps with a meat fork or the back of a spoon as it browns, and then stir it around frequently until all lumps are brown and no pink remains. At that point, it's easy to remove it from the pan with a slotted spoon, and discard the grease from the pan. You can then use the pan again without washing it for any pre-cooking of other ingredients.

CUTTING BACK ON FAT

In addition to cost, another benefit of cooking meat in sauces is that it's possible to remove a great percentage of the saturated fat. It's easy to find and discard this "bad fat," both before and after cooking.

On raw meat, the fat is easy to spot. It's the white stuff around the red stuff. Cut it off with a sharp paring knife, and you're done. However, some fat remains in the tissue of the red meat, and much of this saturated fat is released during the cooking process. There are ways to discard it, when the food is either hot or cold.

If you're cooking in advance and refrigerating a dish, all the fat rises to the top and hardens once chilled. Just scrape it off, throw it away, and you're done. The same principle of fat rising to the surface is true when food is hot, but it's a bit harder to eliminate it. Tilt the pan, and the fat will form a puddle on the lower side. It's then easier to scoop it off with a soup ladle. When you're down to too little to scoop off, level the pan, and blot the top with paper towels.

Grilled Pork Ensalata

This is the pork version of a classic Italian dish traditionally made with veal, in which the meat is topped with what is essentially a tossed salad. It is incredibly refreshing on a summer's day.

Yield: 6 servings | **Active time:** 20 minutes | **Start to finish:** 30 minutes

1¼ pounds boneless pork loin

2 teaspoons Italian seasoning

Salt and freshly ground black pepper to taste

¼ cup balsamic vinegar

2 garlic cloves, peeled and minced

1 teaspoon dried oregano

2 tablespoons olive oil

6 ripe plum tomatoes, rinsed, cored, seeded, and chopped

1 cup finely chopped iceberg lettuce

2 scallions, white parts and 3 inches of green tops, rinsed, trimmed, and chopped

Vegetable oil spray

1. Light a charcoal or gas grill, or preheat the oven broiler.
2. Cut pork into 6 slices, and pound slices between two sheets of plastic wrap to an even thickness of $\frac{1}{2}$ inch. Spray pork with vegetable oil spray, and sprinkle with Italian seasoning, salt, and pepper. Set aside. Combine vinegar, garlic, oregano, salt, and pepper in a jar with a tight-fitting lid, and shake well. Add olive oil, and shake well again. Set aside.
3. Grill pork for 2–3 minutes per side, uncovered, or until cooked through and no longer pink. Remove pork from the grill, and keep warm.
4. Combine tomatoes, lettuce, and scallions in a mixing bowl. Toss with dressing, and season to taste with salt and pepper. To serve, top each cutlet with a portion of salad mixture, and serve immediately.

Note: The dressing can be prepared up to 1 day in advance and refrigerated, tightly covered. Allow it to reach room temperature before using.

Each serving contains:
208 calories

83 calories from fat

9 g fat

2 g saturated fat

22 g protein

8 g carbohydrates

Variations:
- Substitute boneless, skinless chicken breasts or turkey cutlets for the pork.
- Add $\frac{1}{2}$ cup chopped kalamata olives to the salad.

Stir-Fried Pork Lo Mein

This is truly your all-in-one dish, complete with some pasta as well as lean pork and a variety of vegetables. Like all Chinese food, it's a great cold nibble, too. So pack it for lunch the next day.

Yield: 6 servings | **Active time:** 25 minutes | **Start to finish:** 30 minutes

- ¼ pound angel hair pasta, broken into 2-inch lengths
- 1 pound boneless pork loin
- ½ cup dried shiitake mushrooms *
- 1 cup boiling water
- 3 tablespoons reduced-sodium soy sauce
- 3 tablespoons dry sherry
- 3 tablespoons Chinese black bean sauce *
- 2 tablespoons oyster sauce *
- 1 tablespoon cornstarch
- 2 tablespoons cold water
- 2 tablespoons Asian sesame oil *
- 4 scallions, white parts and 4 inches of green tops, rinsed, trimmed, and chopped
- 3 garlic cloves, peeled and minced
- 6 cups firmly packed shredded green cabbage
- 2 celery ribs, rinsed, trimmed, and sliced on the diagonal into ¼-inch slices
- 1 large onion, peeled, halved, and cut into ¼-inch slices
- Freshly ground black pepper to taste

1. Bring a large pot of salted water to a boil, and cook pasta until al dente. Drain, and set aside. Trim all fat from pork, and cut into thin slices against the grain. Place stack of slices on its side, and cut into thin ribbons. Set aside.

2. Soak mushrooms in boiling water for 10 minutes, pushing them down into water with the back of a spoon. Drain mushrooms, reserving soaking liquid. Discard mushroom stems, and slice mushrooms. Set aside. Strain soaking liquid through a sieve lined with a paper coffee filter or a paper towel. Combine soaking liquid with soy sauce, sherry, black bean sauce, and oyster sauce. Stir well, and set aside. Combine cornstarch and cold water in a small cup. Stir well, and set aside.

* Available in the Asian aisle of most supermarkets and in specialty markets.

3. Heat sesame oil in a wok or large skillet over medium-high heat, swirling to coat the pan. Add scallions and garlic, and stir-fry for 30 seconds, or until fragrant. Add pork, and stir-fry for 2 minutes, or until pork loses its pink color. Remove pork from the wok with a slotted spoon, and set aside.

4. Add cabbage, celery, and onion, and stir-fry for 1 minute. Add sauce mixture, and cook for 4–5 minutes, or until vegetables are crisp-tender. Return pork to the wok, and cook for an additional 2 minutes. Stir in cornstarch mixture, and cook for 1 minute, or until slightly thickened. Stir in cooked pasta, and reheat. Season to taste with pepper, and serve immediately.

Note: The pasta can be cooked and the other foods can be prepped up to 4 hours in advance and refrigerated, tightly covered. Do not cook the dish until just prior to serving.

Each serving contains:
303 calories
82 calories from fat
9 g fat
2 g saturated fat
23 g protein
31 g carbohydrates

Variations:
- Substitute light firm tofu for the pork.
- Substitute thinly sliced flank steak or sirloin tips for the pork.
- Substitute boneless, skinless chicken breast for the pork.
- Add 1–2 teaspoons Chinese chile paste with garlic * for a spicier dish.

Spicy Pork in Garlic Sauce

The entrance of fiery Szechwan cooking into Chinese-American restaurants in the late 1960s was a revelation. Suddenly delicate Cantonese dishes were being joined on menus by dishes like this, which are loaded with assertive flavors, and need some brown rice to soak up the sauce.

Yield: 6 servings | **Active time:** 25 minutes | **Start to finish:** 25 minutes

1 pound boneless pork loin
1/4 cup reduced-sodium soy sauce, divided
1/4 cup dry sherry, divided
6 garlic cloves, peeled and minced
3 tablespoons grated fresh ginger
1/2–1 teaspoon crushed red pepper flakes, or to taste
1 teaspoon Asian sesame oil *
1 tablespoon cornstarch
1/2 cup water
1/4 cup hoisin sauce *
1 tablespoon vegetable oil
3 carrots, peeled and thinly sliced on the diagonal
3 celery ribs, rinsed, trimmed, and thinly sliced on the diagonal
6 scallions, white parts and 5 inches of green tops, rinsed, trimmed, and sliced

1. Rinse pork and pat dry with paper towels. Trim all visible fat, and cut pork against the grain into slices 1/8 inch thick. Stack slices, and cut into thin ribbons. Combine 2 tablespoons soy sauce, 2 tablespoons dry sherry, garlic, ginger, red pepper flakes, sesame oil, and cornstarch in a mixing bowl. Stir well, add pork, and toss to coat evenly. Set aside.

2. Combine remaining soy sauce, remaining sherry, water, and hoisin sauce in a small bowl. Stir well, and set aside.

3. Heat oil in a wok or large skillet over high heat, swirling to coat the pan. Add pork, carrot, and celery and stir-fry for 2 minutes, or until slices separate and are no longer red. Add scallions, and stir-fry 1 minute. Add sauce and stir-fry 2 minutes, or until slightly thickened. Serve immediately.

Note: The ingredients for this dish can be prepped up to 6 hours in advance and refrigerated, tightly covered. Do not cook the dish until just prior to serving.

Each serving contains:
190 calories
45 calories from fat
5 g fat
1 g saturated fat
20 g protein
14 g carbohydrates

Variation:
- Substitute boneless, skinless chicken breasts for the pork.

All meats slice better into thin slices if the meat is partially frozen. Rinse the meat, pat it dry, and wrap it in plastic wrap. Freeze it for 15 minutes for thin cuts like chicken breasts, or 45 minutes–1 hour for thick pork loin.

Traditional New Mexican Pozole

This should be called "short-cut pozole" because it uses canned hominy, thus skipping the laborious process of soaking and cooking the whole kernels. Pozole is popular all through New Mexico, and it's savory without being spicy.

Yield: 6 servings | **Active time:** 20 minutes | **Start to finish:** 1 ²/₃ hours

1¼ pounds boneless pork loin
Salt and freshly ground black pepper to taste
2 tablespoons olive oil
1 large onion, peeled and diced
3 garlic cloves, peeled and minced
2 teaspoons ground cumin
2 teaspoons dried oregano
2 cups Chicken Stock (recipe on page 40) or purchased stock
1 (14.5-ounce) can diced tomatoes, undrained
1 (4-ounce) can diced mild green chiles, drained
2 (15-ounce) cans yellow hominy, drained and rinsed well
3 medium yams, peeled and cut into ½-inch dice
1 (10-ounce) package frozen cut green beans, thawed
1 (10-ounce) package frozen corn, thawed
4 scallions, white parts and 3 inches of green tops, rinsed,
   trimmed, and thinly sliced
¼ cup chopped fresh cilantro
Plain nonfat yogurt and lime wedges (optional)

1. Preheat the oven to 350°F. Rinse pork and pat dry with paper towels. Trim pork of all visible fat. Cut pork into 1-inch cubes, and sprinkle with salt and pepper. Heat oil in an ovenproof Dutch oven over medium-high heat, swirling to coat the pan. Add pork cubes in a single layer and cook, turning pieces with tongs, until browned on all sides. Remove pork cubes with tongs, and set aside.

2. Add onion and garlic to the Dutch oven and cook, stirring frequently, for 3 minutes, or until onion is translucent. Stir in cumin and oregano and cook, stirring constantly, for 1 minute. Add pork cubes, chicken stock, tomatoes, and green chiles. Bring to a boil on top of the stove, cover, place the Dutch oven in the oven, and bake for 45 minutes. Add hominy and yams, and bake for an additional 45 minutes.

3. Add green beans, corn, and scallions, and bake an additional 20 minutes, or until pork is very tender. Season to taste with salt and pepper, sprinkle with cilantro, and serve immediately, passing bowls of yogurt and lime wedges, if using.

Note: The dish can be prepared up to 2 days in advance and refrigerated, tightly covered. Reheat it, covered, in a 350°F oven for 20–25 minutes, or until hot.

Each serving contains:
544 calories
110 calories from fat
12 g fat
3 g saturated fat
32 g protein
76 g carbohydrates

Variation:
- Substitute 1¼ pounds boneless, skinless chicken thighs for the pork.

Key West Pork Salad with Oranges

The cooking in the Florida Keys is a combination of American and Cuban with some Caribbean accents thrown in for good measure. This refreshing salad is typical of the use of colorful and flavorful fruits and vegetables found in the Keys.

Yield: 6 servings | **Active time:** 20 minutes | **Start to finish:** 40 minutes

1¼ pounds boneless pork loin
1 teaspoon ground ginger
1 teaspoon dry mustard
1 teaspoon ground coriander
Salt and cayenne to taste
4 navel oranges
¼ cup cider vinegar
2 tablespoons chopped fresh cilantro
2 garlic cloves, peeled and minced
Freshly ground black pepper to taste
¼ cup olive oil
6 cups bite-sized pieces romaine or iceberg lettuce, rinsed and dried
½ small red onion, peeled and thinly sliced
1 small carrot, peeled and shredded
1 celery rib, rinsed, trimmed, and sliced

1. Preheat the oven to 450°F, and line a baking pan with aluminum foil. Rinse pork, and pat dry with paper towels. Trim pork of all visible fat, and cut in half lengthwise into 2 long pieces. Combine ginger, mustard, coriander, salt, and cayenne in a small bowl. Rub mixture onto all sides of pork.

2. Roast pork for 20 minutes, or until an instant-read thermometer registers 145°F. Remove pork from the oven, and allow it to rest for 15 minutes. Then slice pork into thin slices.

3. While pork roasts, prepare salad. Cut all rind and white pith off oranges, and slice thinly. Combine vinegar, cilantro, garlic, salt, and pepper in a jar with a tight-fitting lid. Shake well, add oil, and shake well again.

4. To serve, toss lettuce with onion, carrot, and celery in a mixing bowl, and arrange salad on individual plates or a large platter. Arrange pork and oranges on top, and drizzle with dressing. Serve immediately.

Note: The dressing and the pork can be prepared up to 2 hours in advance and kept at room temperature. The salad ingredients can also be prepared at that time, and should be refrigerated.

Each serving contains:
233 calories
84 calories from fat
9 g fat
2 g saturated fat
22 g protein
16 g carbohydrates

Variation:
- Boneless, skinless chicken breasts or chicken thighs can be substituted for the pork. Roast them at 400°F for 25–30 minutes, or until an instant-read thermometer registers 170°F.

Pork Chops with Chutney

Chutney is a wonderful low-calorie sauce for foods; it's sweet-sour-spicy flavor profile and range of succulent ingredients work with a variety of foods—including these lean pork chops. Serve this with a steamed green vegetable, and perhaps a slice of crusty whole-wheat bread.

Yield: 6 servings | **Active time:** 25 minutes | **Start to finish:** 45 minutes

1¼ pounds boneless pork loin
Salt and freshly ground black pepper to taste
1 tablespoon vegetable oil
1 small onion, peeled and diced
2 garlic cloves, peeled and minced
1 Golden Delicious apple, cored and chopped
1 (14.5-ounce) can diced tomatoes, undrained
¼ cup chopped dried apricots
2 tablespoons raisins
2 tablespoons cider vinegar
2 tablespoons firmly packed dark brown sugar
½ teaspoon hot red pepper sauce, or to taste

1. Preheat the oven to 350°F, and line a 9 x 13-inch baking dish with aluminum foil. Rinse pork and pat dry with paper towels. Trim pork of all visible fat, and cut pork into 6 slices. Pound slices between two sheets of plastic wrap to an even thickness of ½ inch.
2. Sprinkle pork chops with salt and pepper. Heat oil in a large skillet over medium-high heat, swirling to coat the pan. Add pork chops and cook for 1–2 minutes per side, or until browned; this may have to be done in batches. Transfer pork to the baking dish.
3. Add onion and garlic to the skillet, and cook, stirring frequently, for 3 minutes, or until onion is translucent. Add apple, tomatoes, apricots, raisins, vinegar, brown sugar, and hot red pepper sauce to the skillet. Cook, stirring frequently, for 5–7 minutes, or until vegetables are soft and mixture has slightly thickened. Season to taste with salt and pepper.
4. Pour sauce over pork, and bake, covered with foil, for 10–15 minutes, or until pork is cooked through. Serve immediately.

Note: The dish can be prepared up to 2 days in advance and refrigerated, tightly covered. Reheat it, covered, in a 350°F oven for 20–25 minutes, or until hot.

Each serving contains:
212 calories
42 calories from fat
5 g fat
1 g saturated fat
24 g protein
19 g carbohydrates

Variation:
- Substitute boneless, skinless chicken thighs for the pork, and increase the baking time to 30–40 minutes, or until chicken is cooked through and no longer pink.

Brown sugar is refined sugar flavored with molasses. If you're on a low-calorie diet, you may not have it in the pantry, so add 1 teaspoon molasses to refined sugar for this recipe.

Pork Ragu

This Italian dish is a cross between a sauce and a stew. It goes wonderfully over pasta, and the flavors meld especially well with nutty whole-wheat pasta. Or you can just enjoy it out of a bowl like a bowl of chili.

Yield: 6 servings | **Active time:** 20 minutes | **Start to finish:** 1 hour

½ cup dried mushrooms

1 cup boiling water

2 tablespoons olive oil, divided

1 pound lean ground pork

1 pound fresh mushrooms, wiped with a damp paper towel, trimmed, and sliced

2 medium carrots, peeled and sliced

2 medium onions, peeled and diced

2 celery ribs, rinsed, trimmed, and sliced

3 garlic cloves, peeled and minced

5 cups Chicken Stock (recipe on page 40) or purchased stock

3 tablespoons tomato paste

3 tablespoons chopped fresh parsley

1 tablespoon dried rosemary, crumbled

2 teaspoons dried oregano

1 tablespoon cornstarch

2 tablespoons cold water

Salt and freshly ground black pepper to taste

1. Soak dried mushrooms in boiling water, pushing them down into water with the back of a spoon. Allow mushrooms to soak for 10 minutes, then drain, reserving soaking liquid. Discard stems and chop mushrooms. Strain soaking liquid through a sieve lined with a paper coffee filter or a paper towel. Set aside.

2. Heat 1 tablespoon oil in a Dutch oven over medium-high heat, swirling to coat the pan. Add pork, and cook for 5 minutes, breaking up lumps with a fork, or until pork browns. Remove pork from the pan with a slotted spoon, and drain on paper towels. Set aside.

3. Add remaining oil to the pan, and add fresh mushrooms, carrots, onions, celery, and garlic. Cook over medium-high heat, stirring frequently, for 5 minutes, or until mushrooms soften. Return pork to the pan, and add chopped dried mushrooms, mushroom soaking liquid, stock, tomato paste, parsley, rosemary, and oregano. Stir well.

4. Bring to a boil over medium-high heat, then reduce the heat to low, and simmer sauce, uncovered, for 40–50 minutes, or until reduced by $\frac{1}{2}$. Mix cornstarch and water in a small cup, and add to sauce. Simmer 2 minutes, or until slightly thickened. Season to taste with salt and pepper, and serve immediately.

Note: The sauce can be prepared up to 2 days in advance and refrigerated, tightly covered. Reheat it over low heat, stirring occasionally, until hot.

Each serving contains:
308 calories
156 calories from fat
17 g fat
5.5 g saturated fat
21 g protein
19 g carbohydrates

Variation:
- Substitute ground turkey for the pork.

Pork is much more delicate in flavor and lighter in color than beef or lamb, so use chicken stock rather than beef stock for all pork dishes. Beef stock would darken the delicate color and overpower the subtle flavor of pork. Pork is rarely, if ever, made into a stock on its own, although smoked ham bones can be used to flavor stocks and soups.

Japanese Pork Balls on Wilted Spinach

This moist, succulent dish—a variation on Chinese lion's head—is lightly seasoned with Asian overtones to allow the delicate flavors of the ingredients to emerge. The pork balls can be served on plates or passed as hors d'oeuvres on toothpicks, omitting the spinach.

Yield: 6 servings | **Active time:** 15 minutes | **Start to finish:** 40 minutes

- 3 cups water
- 6 large dried shiitake mushrooms *
- 1/3 cup long-grain white rice
- 2 tablespoons Asian sesame oil, divided *
- 1/2 pound mushrooms, wiped with a damp paper towel, trimmed, and chopped
- 4 scallions, white parts and 3 inches of green tops, rinsed, trimmed, and chopped
- 2 garlic cloves, peeled and minced
- 1 tablespoon grated fresh ginger
- 1 pound ground pork
- 2 tablespoons reduced-sodium soy sauce
- Salt and freshly ground black pepper to taste
- 2 (10-ounce) packages frozen leaf spinach, thawed
- 1 tablespoon rice vinegar
- Vegetable oil spray

1. Preheat the oven to 375°F, line a baking pan with aluminum foil, and grease the foil with vegetable oil spray.
2. Bring water to a boil over high heat. Pour off 1 cup into a small bowl, and add dried mushrooms, pushing them down into liquid with the back of a spoon. Allow mushrooms to soak for 10 minutes, then drain and squeeze dry. Discard stems, and coarsely chop caps. Place mushrooms in a mixing bowl.
3. Add rice to remaining boiling water, lower the heat to a simmer, and cook rice, uncovered, for 15 minutes, or until cooked but not mushy. Drain rice in a sieve, rinse with cold water, and add to the mixing bowl.
4. While rice cooks, heat 1 tablespoon oil in a large skillet over medium heat, swirling to coat the pan. Add fresh mushrooms, scallions, garlic,

* Available in the Asian aisle of most supermarkets and in specialty markets.

and ginger. Cook, stirring frequently, for 5 minutes, or until mush-rooms are soft.

5. Scrape mixture into the mixing bowl, add pork and soy sauce, and season to taste with salt and pepper. Form mixture into 24 balls, and arrange them on the prepared pan; spray tops with vegetable oil spray. Bake for 20 minutes, or until cooked through.

6. While meatballs bake, place spinach in a colander, and press with the back of a spoon to extract as much liquid as possible. Heat remaining oil in a skillet, and add spinach. Cook for 2 minutes, stirring occasionally. Sprinkle with vinegar, and season to taste with salt and pepper. To serve, divide spinach among plates and set 4 pork balls on top.

Note: The meat mixture can be made 1 day in advance and refrigerated, tightly covered. Bake the balls and heat the spinach just prior to serving.

Each serving contains:
332 calories
187 calories from fat
21 g fat
7 g saturated fat
20 g protein
19 g carbohydrates

Variation:
- Add 1–2 tablespoons Chinese chile paste with garlic to the meatballs for a spicy dish.

Lasagna Rolls

I promised you there would be hearty dishes in this chapter, and this one certainly qualifies! It has all the components of a traditional Italian lasagna, but using ingredients that are lower in fat, and far less pasta. Toss a salad, and you're ready to go!

Yield: 6 servings | **Active time:** 20 minutes | **Start to finish:** 1½ hours

6 lasagna noodles

½ pound mild or spicy bulk Italian sausage

½ pound mushrooms, wiped with a damp paper towel, trimmed, and thinly sliced

3 garlic cloves, peeled and minced

2½ cups Herbed Tomato Sauce (recipe on page 38) or purchased marinara sauce, divided

Salt and freshly ground black pepper to taste

1 (10-ounce) package frozen chopped spinach, thawed

1 cup low-fat ricotta cheese

1 large egg, lightly beaten

2 teaspoons Italian seasoning

½ cup grated part-skim mozzarella cheese

¼ cup freshly grated Parmesan cheese

Vegetable oil spray

1. Preheat the oven to 375°F, and grease a 9 x 13-inch baking pan with vegetable oil spray. Bring a large pot of salted water to a boil, and cook lasagna noodles according to package directions. Drain noodles, and rinse under cold running water. Set aside in a single layer on a sheet of plastic wrap.

2. Place sausage in a large skillet over medium-high heat. Cook, breaking up lumps with a fork, for 5 minutes, or until sausage browns and no pink remains. Remove sausage from the skillet with a slotted spoon, and drain on paper towels. Discard fat from the skillet.

3. Add mushrooms and garlic to the skillet, and cook for 5 minutes, stirring frequently, or until mushrooms soften. Return sausage to the skillet, and add 1 cup tomato sauce. Bring to a boil, reduce the heat to low, and simmer mixture, uncovered, for 5 minutes. Season to taste with salt and pepper, and set aside.

4. Place spinach in a colander, and press with the back of a spoon to remove as much liquid as possible. Combine spinach, ricotta, egg,

and Italian seasoning in a mixing bowl, and stir well. Season to taste with salt and pepper, and set aside.

5. Spread ½ of remaining tomato sauce on the bottom of the prepared pan. Divide both spinach filling and sausage mixture onto the noodles. Roll each noodle, and transfer them to the baking pan with a spatula. Spread remaining sauce on top of noodles, and then sprinkle mozzarella and Parmesan cheeses.

6. Bake lasagna, lightly covered with aluminum foil, for 30 minutes. Remove the foil, and bake for an additional 15 minutes, or until bubbly. Allow to sit for 5 minutes, then serve.

Note: The dish can be prepared up to 2 days in advance and refrigerated, tightly covered. Reheat it, covered, in a 350°F oven for 20–25 minutes, or until hot.

Each serving contains:
364 calories
156 calories from fat
17 g fat
8 g saturated fat
23 g protein
32 g carbohydrates

Variations:
- Substitute turkey sausage or ground turkey for the pork sausage.
- Make the dish vegetarian by omitting the sausage and adding 1 cup cooked bulgur to the tomato sauce.

Stuffed Peppers with Sausage and Egg

This easy dish can be served as an elegant brunch as well as for supper. Italian sausage simmered in tomato sauce is topped with an egg, and then a whole pepper becomes an edible serving vehicle. A tossed salad goes well with it, as does a grilled vegetable salad.

Yield: 6 servings | **Active time:** 15 minutes | **Start to finish:** 45 minutes

6 small green bell peppers that sit evenly when placed on a flat surface
1 tablespoon olive oil
¼ cup Italian breadcrumbs
½ pound bulk sweet Italian sausage
½ cup marinara sauce
2 tablespoons chopped fresh parsley
1 teaspoon Italian seasoning
6 large eggs
Salt and freshly ground black pepper to taste
3 tablespoons freshly grated Parmesan cheese
Vegetable oil spray

1. Bring a large pot of salted water to a boil over high heat. Preheat the oven to 375°F, and grease a 9 x 13-inch baking pan with vegetable oil spray.
2. Cut tops off peppers. Discard tops and seeds, and pull out ribs with your fingers. Boil peppers for 4 minutes. Remove peppers from water with tongs, and place upside down on paper towels to drain.
3. While peppers blanch, heat olive oil in a heavy skillet over medium heat, swirling to coat the pan. Add breadcrumbs and cook, stirring constantly, for 2 minutes, or until brown. Scrape crumbs into a small bowl, and set aside. In the same pan, cook sausage over medium-high heat, breaking up lumps with a fork. Cook sausage, stirring frequently, for 5 minutes, or until brown with no trace of pink. Remove sausage from the pan with a slotted spoon, and drain on paper towels. Discard all grease from the pan. Return sausage to the pan, and add marinara sauce, parsley, and Italian seasoning. Bring to a boil, reduce the heat to low, and simmer mixture, stirring occasionally, for 10 minutes.
4. Place peppers into the prepared pan. Evenly divide sausage mixture into the bottom of each pepper. Break 1 egg on top of sausage, and

sprinkle eggs with salt and pepper, toasted breadcrumbs, and Parmesan cheese.

5. Bake peppers for 20 minutes, or until egg whites are set. Serve immediately.

Note: The peppers can be prepared for baking up to 2 hours in advance and kept at room temperature. Bake them just prior to serving.

Each serving contains:
276 calories
167 calories from fat
19 g fat
7 g saturated fat
17 g protein
12 g carbohydrates

Variation:
- Substitute ground turkey or turkey sausage for the Italian sausage.

Chinese Beef Stew

Every culture and cuisine has stews; in China they're called sand-pots because of the ceramic casseroles in which they're baked. The vegetables are added to this stew late into the cooking process, so they remain crisp.

Yield: 6 servings | **Active time:** 20 minutes | **Start to finish:** 2³/₄ hours

1 pound lean stewing beef
1 tablespoon Asian sesame oil *
3 scallions, white parts and 3 inches of green tops, rinsed, trimmed, and thinly sliced
2 tablespoons grated fresh ginger
4 garlic cloves, peeled and minced
2 cups Beef Stock (recipe on page 41) or purchased stock
¼ cup dry sherry
3 tablespoons reduced-sodium soy sauce
2 tablespoons Chinese oyster sauce *
1 tablespoon firmly packed dark brown sugar
¼–½ teaspoon crushed red pepper flakes
1 teaspoon Chinese five-spice powder *
³/₄ pound mushrooms, wiped with a damp paper towel, trimmed, and sliced
½ pound peeled baby carrots
3 cups firmly packed shredded cabbage
1 (10-ounce) package frozen sliced green beans, thawed
Salt and freshly ground black pepper to taste
1 tablespoon cornstarch
2 tablespoons cold water

1. Preheat the oven to 350°F. Rinse beef, and pat dry with paper towels.

2. Heat oil in an ovenproof Dutch oven over medium-high heat, swirling to coat the pan. Add beef cubes to the pan, being careful not to crowd the pan. Turn beef with tongs to brown on all sides. Remove beef from the pan with a slotted spoon, and set aside. Add scallions, ginger, and garlic to the pan. Cook, stirring constantly, for 1 minute.

* Available in the Asian aisle of most supermarkets and in specialty markets.

3. Return beef to the pan and stir in stock, sherry, soy sauce, oyster sauce, brown sugar, crushed red pepper flakes, and five-spice powder. Bring to a boil on top of the stove, then cover the pan and transfer it to the oven. Bake for 2¼ hours.

4. Add mushrooms, carrots, and cabbage to stew. Bring to a boil on top of the stove, and then return the pan to the oven. Bake for 20 minutes. Add green beans, and bake for 5 minutes more. Season to taste with salt and pepper.

5. Combine cornstarch and water in a small bowl. Remove stew from the oven, and place it on the stove over medium-high heat. Add cornstarch mixture, and simmer for 2 minutes, or until slightly thickened. Serve immediately.

Note: The dish can be prepared up to 2 days in advance and refrigerated, tightly covered. Reheat it, covered, in a 350°F oven for 20–25 minutes, or until hot.

Each serving contains:
253 calories
84 calories from fat
9 g fat
3 g saturated fat
22 g protein
19 g carbohydrates

Variation:
- Cubes of pork loin can be substituted for the beef. Reduce the initial cooking time in the oven to 1 hour, and then finish the recipe as instructed.

Oyster sauce is a seasoning staple of the Chinese pantry. It's made from oysters, brine, and soy sauce, and it's cooked until it's deep brown, thick, and concentrated. It gives dishes a rich flavor that's not at all "fishy," and it's not as salty as soy sauce.

Asian Steak Salad

Sirloin tips, the "tails" cut off most steaks, are usually—along with flank steak—the least expensive steaks in the meat case that are still tender enough for a salad such as this one. It's simultaneously hearty and refreshing.

Yield: 6 servings | **Active time:** 20 minutes | **Start to finish:** 1½ hours, including 1 hour for marinating

1 pound sirloin tips
¼ cup rice vinegar
2 tablespoons reduced-sodium soy sauce
2 tablespoons Dijon mustard
2 tablespoons grated fresh ginger
3 garlic cloves, peeled and minced
3 scallions, white parts and 3 inches of green tops, rinsed, trimmed, and chopped
2 teaspoons firmly packed dark brown sugar
1 teaspoon Chinese chile paste with garlic *
2 tablespoons Asian sesame oil *
½ pound green beans, trimmed and cut into 1-inch lengths
6 cups bite-sized pieces of romaine lettuce, rinsed and dried
3 celery ribs, rinsed, trimmed, and thinly sliced on the diagonal
1 large cucumber, peeled, halved, seeded, and thinly sliced
1 green bell pepper, seeds and ribs removed, and thinly sliced

1. Rinse meat, and pat dry with paper towels. Combine vinegar, soy sauce, mustard, ginger, garlic, scallions, brown sugar, and chile paste in a jar with a tight-fitting lid. Shake well. Add oil, and shake well again.

2. Place steak in a heavy resealable plastic bag, and pour in ½ of dressing. Marinate steak at room temperature for 1 hour, turning the bag occasionally.

3. Light a charcoal or gas grill, or preheat the oven broiler. While steak marinates, bring a large pot of salted water to a boil. Add green beans, and cook for 1 minute. Drain, and plunge green beans into ice water to stop the cooking action. Drain again, and set aside.

* Available in the Asian aisle of most supermarkets and in specialty markets.

4. Remove steak from marinade, and discard marinade. Grill or broil steak for 3–4 minutes per side for medium-rare, or to desired doneness. Allow steak to rest for 5 minutes.

5. Combine green beans, lettuce, celery, cucumber, and green bell pepper in a large mixing bowl. Toss with $\frac{1}{2}$ of remaining dressing, and place vegetables on a platter or individual plates. Slice steak thinly, and place on top of vegetables. Serve immediately, passing remaining dressing separately.

Note: The steak can marinate for up to 6 hours, refrigerated, and the remaining dressing can be made at that time and kept at room temperature.

Each serving contains:
205 calories
97 calories from fat
11 g fat
3 g saturated fat
18 g protein
9 g carbohydrates

Variation:
- Substitute 1 pound boneless pork loin, cut into thick slices, for the steak.

Spicy Beef, Pasta, and Mushroom Salad

Here's your all-in-one meal that is representative of "fusion cooking"; it draws elements from both East and West. The cooked mushrooms and stir-fried steak slices form a contrast to the crunchy raw vegetables.

Yield: 6 servings | **Active time:** 20 minutes | **Start to finish:** 50 minutes, including 30 minutes to chill

> 1/3 pound dried angel hair pasta, broken into 2-inch sections
> 1 tablespoon vegetable oil
> 1/2 pound flank steak, trimmed of all fat, and cut into 1/4-inch slices
> 1/2 pound fresh mushrooms, washed, stemmed, and thinly sliced
> 6 scallions, white parts and 3 inches of green tops, rinsed, trimmed, and sliced
> 1 small cucumber, peeled, seeded, and thinly sliced
> 3 tablespoons reduced-sodium soy sauce
> 3 tablespoons balsamic vinegar
> 3 tablespoons rice vinegar
> 1/2 teaspoon crushed red pepper flakes
> 2 garlic cloves, peeled and minced
> 2 teaspoons grated fresh ginger
> 1/2 teaspoon granulated sugar
> Freshly ground black pepper to taste
> 2 tablespoons Asian sesame oil *
> 6 cups shredded iceberg or romaine lettuce, rinsed and dried

1. Bring a large pot of salted water to a boil. Cook pasta according to package directions until al dente. Drain thoroughly, and refrigerate.
2. Heat oil in a heavy wok or skillet over high heat, swirling to coat the pan. Add beef and stir-fry for 1–2 minutes, or until no longer red. Remove beef from the pan with a slotted spoon, and place it the bowl with the pasta. Add mushrooms to the pan, reduce the heat to medium, and stir-fry mushrooms for 5 minutes, stirring constantly. Add mushrooms to the mixing bowl with pasta and beef, and also add scallions and cucumber. Refrigerate for at least 45 minutes, or until cold, covered with plastic wrap.
3. Combine soy sauce, balsamic vinegar, rice vinegar, red pepper flakes, garlic, ginger, sugar, and pepper in a jar with a tight-fitting lid. Shake well, add sesame oil, and shake well again. Toss 2/3 of dressing with

salad. Chill for at least 30 minutes, tossing occasionally to coat all parts of salad with dressing.

4. To serve, arrange lettuce on a platter or individual plates, and top with salad. Serve immediately, passing remaining dressing separately.

Note: The salad can be made up to 1 day in advance and refrigerated, tightly covered.

Each serving contains:
244 calories
84 calories from fat
9 g fat
2 g saturated fat
14 g protein
26 g carbohydrates

Variation:
- Substitute boneless, skinless chicken thighs, cut into thin slices, for the beef. Cook chicken until cooked through and no longer pink before removing it from the pan.

While I'm not a fan of filling the kitchen with gadgets, if you happen to have an egg slicer, use it for slicing mushrooms. It's fast, and the slices will all be the same width.

Low-Cal Sloppy Joes

While the exact origins of this American classic are not known, recipes for this indeed sloppy dish date back to the early 1940s, and by the 1960s it was a fixture in every school cafeteria. This version complements the beef with low-calorie mushrooms.

Yield: 6 servings | **Active time:** 20 minutes | **Start to finish:** 30 minutes

2 teaspoons vegetable oil
½ pound extra-lean ground beef
1 large onion, peeled and diced
2 garlic cloves, peeled and minced
½ green bell pepper, seeds and ribs removed, and chopped
⅓ pound mushrooms, wiped with a damp paper towel, trimmed, and diced
3 tablespoons all-purpose flour
1 tablespoon chili powder
½ cup water
¼ cup ketchup
¼ cup chili sauce
¼ cup cider vinegar
1 tablespoon Dijon mustard
1 (14.5-ounce) can diced tomatoes, drained
Salt and freshly ground black pepper to taste
6 whole-wheat hamburger buns, toasted

1. Heat oil in a large skillet over medium-high heat, swirling to coat the pan. Add beef, and cook, breaking up lumps with a fork, until browned. Remove beef from the pan with a slotted spoon, and drain on paper towels. Set beef aside, and pour grease out of the skillet.

2. Add onion, garlic, green bell pepper, and mushrooms to the skillet. Cook, stirring frequently, for 5–7 minutes, or until mushrooms soften. Stir flour and chili powder into the skillet, and cook for 1 minute, stirring constantly.

3. Return beef to the pan, and stir in water, ketchup, chili sauce, vinegar, mustard, and tomatoes. Stir well, and bring to a boil. Reduce the heat to medium, and simmer mixture, uncovered, stirring occasionally, for 8–10 minutes, or until thickened and vegetables are tender. Season to taste with salt and pepper, and serve immediately, with meat mixture piled onto buns.

Note: The meat mixture can be prepared up to 2 days in advance and refrigerated, tightly covered. Reheat it, covered, over low heat, stirring occasionally.

Each serving contains:
257 calories
51 calories from fat
6 g fat
2 g saturated fat
14.5 g protein
37 g carbohydrates

Variations:
- Add 1/2 cup cooked corn kernels to the meat mixture.
- Substitute 2 medium zucchini squash, rinsed, trimmed, and cut into 1/2-inch dice, for the mushrooms.

Check the calorie counts of condiments like chili sauce and ketchup. Different brands can vary widely.

Veggie-Packed Meatloaf

By "stretching" the meat with vegetables you can get all the heartiness of a meatloaf with a fraction of the calories and fat. The tunnel of spinach in the center creates an attractive presentation for the down-to-earth dish, which is lightly spiced.

Yield: 6 servings | **Active time:** 20 minutes | **Start to finish:** 1½ hours

2 teaspoons vegetable oil
2 medium onions, peeled and finely chopped
2 garlic cloves, peeled and minced
1 carrot, peeled and finely grated
1 pound lean ground beef
¼ cup plain breadcrumbs
1 large egg, lightly beaten
2 large egg whites
2 tablespoons freshly grated Parmesan cheese
2 tablespoons chopped fresh parsley
1 tablespoon paprika
½ teaspoon dried thyme
Salt and freshly ground black pepper to taste
1 (10-ounce) package frozen chopped spinach, thawed
¼ cup grated part-skim mozzarella cheese, grated

1. Preheat the oven to 350°F, and line a baking sheet with aluminum foil.
2. Heat oil in a medium skillet over medium heat, swirling to coat the pan. Add onions, garlic, and carrot, and cook, stirring frequently, for 10–12 minutes, or until onions are soft.
3. Scrape mixture into a mixing bowl, and add beef, breadcrumbs, egg, egg whites, Parmesan cheese, parsley, paprika, thyme, salt, and pepper. Mix well with a wooden spoon or your hands until light in texture. Set aside.
4. Place spinach in a colander, and press with the back of a spoon to extract as much liquid as possible. Mix spinach with mozzarella cheese, and season to taste with salt and pepper.
5. Form ½ of meat into a rectangle about 9 inches long and 4 inches wide on the baking sheet. Make a tunnel of spinach in the center and then top with remaining meat, smoothing the top and sides to form a loaf.

6. Bake for 1 hour, or until an instant-read thermometer registers 160°F. Allow to sit for 5 minutes. Slice, and serve immediately. The meatloaf can also be served cold or at room temperature.

Note: The meatloaf can be made up to 2 days in advance, and refrigerated, tightly covered. Reheat, covered with foil, in a 300°F oven for 20 minutes, and do not slice until ready to serve. Or, it can be assembled 1 day in advance, kept covered with plastic wrap in the refrigerator, and baked just before serving.

Each serving contains:
215 calories
73 calories from fat
8 g fat
3 g saturated fat
23.5 g protein
12.5 g carbohydrates

Variation:
• Substitute ground pork or ground turkey for the ground beef.

Black Bean Chili

Black beans may not be traditional in chili, but I like their earthy flavor more than that of pinto beans. There's a bit of wine in this recipe, too, which adds depth of flavor. Serve it with brown rice, passing bowls of reduced-fat cheddar cheese and nonfat plain yogurt separately.

Yield: 6 servings | **Active time:** 15 minutes | **Start to finish:** 1 hour

1 tablespoon olive oil
3/4 pound lean ground beef
1 medium onion, peeled and diced
1 green bell pepper, seeds and ribs removed, and diced
3 garlic cloves, peeled and minced
3 tablespoons chili powder
1 tablespoon ground cumin
2 teaspoons dried oregano
1 (28-ounce) can crushed tomatoes in tomato puree
1/2 cup dry red wine
1 (4-ounce) can chopped mild green chiles, drained
2 (15-ounce) cans black beans, drained and rinsed
Salt and freshly ground black pepper

1. Heat oil in a saucepan over medium-high heat, swirling to coat the pan. Add beef and cook, breaking up lumps with a fork, until beef is brown and no pink remains. Remove beef from the pan with a slotted spoon, drain on paper towels, and set aside. Discard liquid and fat from the pan.

2. Add onion, green bell pepper, and garlic to the pan. Cook over medium-high heat, stirring frequently, for 3 minutes, or until onion is translucent. Add chili powder, cumin, and oregano to the pan, and cook for 1 minute, stirring constantly. Return beef to the pan, and add tomatoes, wine, and green chiles.

3. Bring to a boil and simmer mixture, partially covered, for 30 minutes, stirring occasionally. Add beans, and simmer for an additional 15 minutes, or until thick and beef is tender. Season to taste with salt and pepper, and serve immediately.

Note: The dish can be cooked up to 2 days in advance and refrigerated, tightly covered. Reheat it over low heat, covered, until hot.

Each serving contains:

339 calories

83 calories from fat

9 g fat

3 g saturated fat

22 g protein

38 g carbohydrates

Variations:

- Substitute ground pork or ground turkey for the beef.
- Substitute ³/₄-inch cubes of firm tofu for the beef; add tofu to the pan at the same time as the beans.
- For spicier chili, substitute 2 chipotle chiles in adobo sauce, finely chopped, for the canned mild green chiles.

This recipe demonstrates one of the principles of low-calorie cooking discussed in Chapter 2. Draining the beef and discarding the fat from the pan reduces the calories, yet there's enough of a thin coating of fat to sauté the vegetables.

Stuffed Zucchini

This is another all-in-one meal; there's some brown rice in the filling along with the zucchini pulp and ground beef. The zucchini are baked in a tomato sauce, enlivened with some Parmesan cheese.

Yield: 6 servings | **Active time:** 20 minutes | **Start to finish:** 1¼ hours

> 6 medium zucchini, rinsed and trimmed
> ½ pound extra-lean ground beef
> 2 tablespoons olive oil
> 1 small onion, peeled and chopped
> 3 garlic cloves, peeled and minced
> 1 cup cooked brown rice
> 2 tablespoons chopped fresh parsley
> 2 teaspoons Italian seasoning
> ⅔ cup grated part-skim mozzarella cheese
> Salt and freshly ground black pepper to taste
> 1 (15-ounce) can tomato sauce
> ¼ cup freshly grated Parmesan cheese

1. Preheat the oven to 375°F, and line a 9 x 13-inch baking dish with aluminum foil.
2. Slice zucchini in half lengthwise, and cut out pulp using a small serrated knife, leaving a ½-inch-thick shell. Chop zucchini flesh, and set aside.
3. Place beef in a large skillet and cook over medium-high heat, breaking up lumps with a fork, for 5 minutes, or until beef is brown and no pink remains. Remove beef from the skillet with a slotted spoon, and drain on paper towels. Discard liquid from the skillet.
4. Heat oil in the skillet over medium-high heat, swirling to coat the pan. Add onion, garlic, and chopped zucchini pulp, and cook, stirring frequently, for 5 minutes, or until vegetables soften. Remove the pan from the heat, and stir in beef, rice, parsley, Italian seasoning, and mozzarella cheese. Season to taste with salt and pepper, and stuff mixture into zucchini shells.
5. Arrange zucchini in the prepared pan. Spoon tomato sauce over top of zucchini, and sprinkle with Parmesan cheese. Cover the pan with aluminum foil, and bake for 20 minutes. Remove the foil, and bake for an additional 30 minutes, or until zucchini is tender. Remove the pan from the oven, and allow to sit for 5 minutes. Serve immediately.

Note: The zucchini can be prepared up to baking 1 day in advance and refrigerated, tightly covered. Add 10 minutes to covered baking time if chilled.

Each serving contains:
226 calories
87 calories from fat
10 g fat
3 g saturated fat
17 g protein
20 g carbohydrates

Variations:
- For a Southwestern dish, substitute cilantro for the parsley, 2 teaspoons ground cumin for the Italian seasoning, and jalapeño Jack for the mozzarella cheese. Then add 2 tablespoons chili powder to the tomato sauce.
- For a spicier dish, substitute spicy Italian sausage for the ground beef.

Chapter 7:
Two If By Sea . . . Fish Entrees

All species of fin fish are the ultimate low-calorie food, and luckily they're becoming nationally accessible at a relatively low cost. While fish is usually higher in price than most meats, there is no waste to a fish fillet, and with its low fat content it doesn't shrink the way that meats do. So the price per edible ounce of fish is really about the same as for other forms of protein like a chuck roast or pork loin, if still more expensive than chicken.

It's more important to use the freshest fish—and one that is reasonably priced—than to use any specific fish species. That's why these recipes are not written for cod, halibut, or pompano. They're written for two generic types of fish—thin white-fleshed fillets and thick white-fleshed fillets. These encompass most types of fish. They are all low in fat, mild to delicate in flavor, and flake easily when cooked. The only species of fish that should not be used in these recipes are tuna, bluefish, and mackerel; they will all be too strong. Salmon, if you find it at a good price, can be substituted for either classification of fish, depending on the thickness of the fillet.

There are thousands of species that fit these rather large definitions. Here are some of the most common:

- Thin fillets: Flounder, sole, perch, red snapper, trout, tilapia, ocean perch, catfish, striped bass, turbot, and whitefish.

- Thick fillets: Halibut, scrod, cod, haddock, grouper, sea bass, mahi-mahi, pompano, yellowtail, and swordfish.

FISH FACTS

Fish are high in protein and low to moderate in fat, cholesterol, and sodium. A 3-ounce portion of fish has between 47 and 170 calories depending on the species. Fish is an excellent source of B vitamins, iodine, phosphorus, potassium, iron, and calcium.

The most important nutrient in fish may be the Omega-3 fatty acids. These are the primary polyunsaturated fatty acids found in the fat and oils of fish. They have been found to lower the levels of low-density lipoproteins (LDL), the "bad" cholesterol, and raise the levels of high-density lipoproteins (HDL), the "good" cholesterol. Fatty fish that live in cold water, such as mackerel and salmon, seem to have the most Omega-3 fatty acids, although all fish have some.

HANDLING THE AQUATICS

Most supermarkets still display fish on chipped ice in a case rather than pre-packaging it, and they should. Fish should be kept at even a lower temperature than meats. Fish fillets or steaks should look bright, lustrous, and moist, with no signs of discoloration or drying.

When making your fish selection, keep a few simple guidelines in mind: above all, do not buy any fish that actually smells fishy, indicating that it is no longer fresh or hasn't been cut or stored properly. Fresh fish has the mild, clean scent of the sea—nothing more. Look for bright, shiny colors in the fish scales, because as a fish sits, its skin becomes more pale and dull looking. Then peer into the eyes; they should be black and beady. If they're milky or sunken, the fish has been dead too long. And if the fish isn't behind glass, gently poke its flesh. If the indentation remains, the fish is old.

Rinse all fish under cold running water before cutting or cooking. With fillets, run your fingers in every direction along the top of the fillet before cooking, feeling for any pesky little bones.

You can remove bones easily in two ways. Larger bones will come out if you stroke them with a vegetable peeler, and you can pull out smaller bones with tweezers. This is not a long process, but it's a gesture that will be greatly appreciated by all who eat the fish.

TALKING TUNA

There is a dizzying array of cans, and now pouches, on supermarket shelves, but they essentially fall into four categories. They are solid white tuna packed in water, solid white tuna packed in oil, light tuna packed in water, or light tuna packed in oil. Obviously water-packed tuna is specified in these recipes because of the calorie content. A can of light tuna packed in oil has 392 calories, after draining, while the water-packed tuna has 199 calories. That's a big difference.

There are health concerns as well as cost reasons for specifying light tuna rather than white tuna, sometimes called albacore tuna, in these recipes. White tuna has been found to be much higher in mercury than light tuna, so light tuna is better on both scores. In any recipe containing canned tuna, feel free to substitute canned salmon. Almost all canned salmon is packaged complete with bones and skin, however, so some preparatory work is needed before using it in recipes.

Rhode Island Clam Chowder

I never tried my adopted state's version of chowder until I moved to Providence in 2003. It's a broth-only chowder; it's not made with any dairy product. It delivers the wonderful flavor of its star, but I also give you a variation that transforms it into a New England chowder.

Yield: 4 servings | **Active time:** 20 minutes | **Start to finish:** 40 minutes

> 1 pint fresh minced clams
> 2 tablespoons unsalted butter, divided
> 2 medium onions, peeled and diced
> 2 celery ribs, rinsed, trimmed, and diced
> 2 (8-ounce) bottles clam juice
> 2 medium redskin potatoes, scrubbed and cut into ½-inch dice
> 2 tablespoons chopped fresh parsley
> 1 bay leaf
> 1 teaspoon dried thyme
> 3 tablespoons all-purpose flour
> Salt and freshly ground black pepper to taste

1. Drain clams in a sieve over a mixing bowl, reserving juice in the bowl. Press down with the back of a spoon to extract as much liquid as possible from clams.
2. Melt 1 tablespoon butter in a large saucepan over medium heat. Add onions and celery, and cook, stirring frequently, for 3 minutes, or until onions are translucent. Add bottled clam juice and reserved clam juice to the pan, along with potatoes, parsley, bay leaf, and thyme. Bring to a boil, reduce the heat to low, and simmer, covered, for 12 minutes, or until potatoes are tender.
3. While mixture simmers, melt remaining butter in a small saucepan over low heat. Stir in flour and cook, stirring constantly, for 2 minutes. Add flour mixture and clams to chowder. Bring to a boil, reduce the heat, and simmer, uncovered, for 3 minutes. Remove and discard

bay leaf, season chowder to taste with salt and pepper, and serve immediately.

Note: The chowder can be made up to 2 days in advance and refrigerated, tightly covered. Reheat it over low heat, stirring occasionally.

Each serving contains:
304 calories
60 calories from fat
7 g fat
3 g saturated fat
19 g protein
42 g carbohydrates

Variations:
- Add 1 cup cooked corn kernels along with the clams to the chowder.
- Substitute 1 cup whole milk for 1 bottle of clam juice for a New England chowder that will still be moderately low in calories.

Manhattan Clam Chowder

Manhattan chowder is really a tomato vegetable soup with clams, which means that it is very low in calories while still being filling. I like it served with coleslaw rather than a tossed salad.

Yield: 4 servings | **Active time:** 20 minutes | **Start to finish:** 40 minutes

1 pint fresh minced clams
1 tablespoon olive oil
1 medium onion, peeled and diced
$\frac{1}{2}$ green bell pepper, seeds and ribs removed, and chopped
2 celery ribs, rinsed, trimmed, and sliced
2 medium redskin potatoes, scrubbed and cut into $\frac{1}{3}$-inch dice
2 (8-ounce) bottles clam juice
1 (14.5-ounce) can diced tomatoes, preferably petite diced, undrained
3 tablespoons chopped fresh parsley
1 bay leaf
1 teaspoon dried thyme
Salt and freshly ground black pepper to taste

1. Drain clams in a sieve over a mixing bowl, reserving juice in the bowl. Press down with the back of a spoon to extract as much liquid as possible from clams.
2. Heat oil in a heavy large saucepan over medium-high heat, swirling to coat the pan. Add onion, green bell pepper, and celery. Cook, stirring frequently, for 3 minutes, or until onion is translucent.
3. Add potatoes, juice from fresh clams, bottled clam juice, tomatoes, parsley, and thyme to the pan. Bring to a boil, reduce the heat to low, and simmer for 10 minutes, stirring occasionally, or until potatoes are tender. Add clams, bring soup back to a boil, and simmer for 5 minutes. Remove and discard bay leaf, season to taste with salt and pepper, and serve immediately.

Note: The soup can be made up to 2 days in advance and refrigerated, tightly covered. Reheat over low heat, stirring occasionally, and do not allow it to boil or the clams will toughen.

Each serving contains:

269 calories

37 calories from fat

4 g fat

0.5 g saturated fat

19 g protein

39.5 g carbohydrates

Variations:

- To add some Southwestern flavor, substitute 2 tablespoons chili powder, 2 teaspoons ground cumin, and 1 teaspoon dried oregano for the thyme, and substitute chopped cilantro for the parsley.
- Substitute ¾-pound thin white-fleshed fish fillets, cut into ½-inch cubes, for the clams.

Bay leaves, also called bay laurel or sweet bay in some cookbooks, add both flavor and aroma to dishes. But their flavor is extremely bitter if chewed, which is why they are always removed.

Asian Mussels in Black Bean Sauce

Mussels remain an affordable mollusk, while clams and oysters are almost always priced beyond the guidelines of this book. This is an authentic Chinese way to prepare them, and I usually spoon the resulting sauce over some brown rice.

Yield: 6 servings | **Active time:** 15 minutes | **Start to finish:** 20 minutes

4 pounds live mussels
2 tablespoons Chinese fermented black beans, coarsely chopped *
$\frac{1}{3}$ cup dry sherry
2 teaspoons Asian sesame oil *
8 scallions, white parts and 4 inches of green tops, rinsed, trimmed, and thinly sliced, divided
4 garlic cloves, peeled and minced
2 tablespoons grated fresh ginger
2 tablespoons reduced-sodium soy sauce

1. Just before cooking, clean mussels by scrubbing them well with a brush under cold water; discard any that do not shut tightly. Scrape off any barnacles with a knife. If beard is still attached, remove it by pulling it from tip to hinge, or by pulling and cutting it off with a knife. Set aside. Stir black beans into sherry to plump for 10 minutes.

2. Heat oil in a large skillet over medium-high heat, swirling to coat the pan. Add $\frac{1}{2}$ of scallions, garlic, and ginger. Cook, stirring constantly, for 30 seconds, or until fragrant. Add mussels, sherry mixture, and soy sauce. Cover the pan and bring to a boil over high heat. Steam mussels for 3 minutes, stir to redistribute seafood, and steam for an additional 2–3 minutes, or until mussels open. Discard any mussels that do not open, and remove the pan from the heat.

3. Divide mussels into low bowls, and top each serving with broth from the skillet. Sprinkle each serving with remaining scallions, and serve immediately, with soup spoons as well as seafood forks.

Note: The mussels can also be served at room temperature or cold.

* Available in the Asian aisle of most supermarkets and in specialty markets.

Each serving contains:

316 calories

76 calories from fat

8.5 g fat

1.5 g saturated fat

38 g protein

16 g carbohydrates

Variations:

- For a spicier dish, add ½–1 teaspoon crushed red pepper flakes along with mussels to the skillet.
- Substitute small littleneck clams for the mussels, if you can find them on sale.

Mussels and clams must be alive and fresh when cooked, and they give us two chances to practice food safety. The first is before they're cooked; they should shut tightly if you pinch them. And the second chance to cull out potential problems is after steaming. If they didn't pop open, discard them.

Garlicky Steamed Mussels

This is a linguine with mussel sauce without the linguine, but feel free to put some linguine or other whole-wheat pasta on the bottom of your bowl. It's one of the fastest and most flavorful dinners you can put on the table.

Yield: 6 servings | **Active time:** 10 minutes | **Start to finish:** 15 minutes

> 4 pounds live mussels
> 2 tablespoons olive oil
> 6 garlic cloves, peeled and minced
> ¼ cup water
> ¼ cup dry white wine
> ¼ cup chopped fresh parsley
> 2 teaspoons Italian seasoning
> Salt and freshly ground black pepper to taste

1. Just before cooking, clean mussels by scrubbing them well with a brush under cold water; discard any that do not shut tightly. Scrape off any barnacles with a knife. If beard is still attached, remove it by pulling it from tip to hinge, or by pulling and cutting it off with a knife. Set aside.

2. Heat olive oil in a large skillet over medium heat, swirling to coat the pan. Add garlic and cook, stirring frequently, for 2 minutes. Raise the heat to high and add water, wine, parsley, Italian seasoning, and mussels. Cover the pan and bring to a boil over high heat. Steam mussels for 3 minutes, stir to redistribute seafood, and steam for an additional 2–3 minutes, or until mussels open. Discard any mussels that do not open, and remove the pan from the heat.

3. Remove mussels from the pan with a slotted spoon, and season broth to taste with salt and pepper. To serve, place mussels in shallow bowls and ladle broth on top. Serve with soup spoons as well as seafood forks.

Note: The mussels can also be served at room temperature or cold.

Each serving contains:
298 calories
92 calories from fat
10 g fat
2 g saturated fat
36 g protein
12 g carbohydrates

Variations:
- For a Latino dish, substitute cilantro for the parsley and 2 table-spoons chili powder for the Italian seasoning, and add 1 finely chopped chipotle chile in adobo sauce along with the liquids.
- Substitute small littleneck clams for the mussels, if you can find them on sale.

> If there's broth left over from a recipe for steamed mollusks it's a treasure trove of flavor for saucing future fish dishes—and it's free. Freeze it, and make sure to mark what it's from so you know what flavors you're adding.

Asian Stir-Fried Fish and Vegetables

Fish is treated with light seasonings in this delicate dish that contains all the vegetables you need for dinner, too. Serve it over some brown rice with a cup of green tea, if not white wine.

Yield: 6 servings | **Active time:** 25 minutes | **Start to finish:** 25 minutes

1½ pounds thin white-fleshed fish fillets, cut into 1-inch cubes
12 dried shiitake mushrooms
1 cup boiling water
½ cup dry sherry
3 tablespoons reduced-sodium soy sauce
3 tablespoons lime juice
2 teaspoons granulated sugar
2 tablespoons cold water
1 tablespoon cornstarch
2 tablespoons Asian sesame oil *
3 tablespoons grated fresh ginger
4 garlic cloves, peeled and minced
4 scallions, white parts and 4 inches of green tops, rinsed, trimmed and cut into 1-inch lengths
2 celery ribs, rinsed, trimmed, and sliced
1 green bell pepper, seeds and ribs removed, cut into thin strips
¼ pound mushrooms, wiped with a damp paper towel, trimmed, and sliced
¼ pound fresh green beans, rinsed, trimmed, and cut into 1-inch lengths
Salt and freshly ground black pepper to taste

1. Rinse fish and pat dry with paper towels. Soak shiitake mushrooms in boiling water for 10 minutes, pushing them down with the back of a spoon. Drain mushrooms, squeezing to remove excess water. Discard mushroom stems, and chop coarsely. Set aside. Combine sherry, soy sauce, lime juice, and sugar in a small bowl. Stir well, and set aside. Combine cold water and cornstarch in a small bowl. Stir well, and set aside.

2. Heat oil in a wok or large skillet over high heat, swirling to coat the pan. Add ginger and garlic, and stir-fry, stirring constantly, for 30

* Available in the Asian aisle of most supermarkets and in specialty markets.

seconds, or until fragrant. Add fish, and cook for 1 minute. Remove fish from the pan with a slotted spoon, and set aside. Add scallions, celery, green bell pepper, fresh mushrooms, and soaked shiitake mushrooms.

3. Stir-fry vegetables for 2 minutes, stirring constantly. Return fish to the pan and add green beans and sauce mixture. Bring to a boil and simmer for 2 minutes, then stir in cornstarch mixture. Simmer 1 minute, or until slightly thickened, and season to taste with salt and pepper. Serve immediately.

Note: All the ingredients can be prepped up to 4 hours in advance and refrigerated, tightly covered.

Each serving contains:
230 calories
52 calories from fat
6 g fat
1 g saturated fat
25 g protein
17 g carbohydrates

Variation:
- Substitute 1-inch cubes of light firm tofu for the fish for a vegetarian dish.

An easy way to rehydrate mushrooms, or any dry ingredient, is in a French press coffee maker. Place the ingredients and liquid in the pot, and lower the top to keep the ingredients submerged. If you're saving the soaking liquid for any reason, the mesh on the top will also serve as a strainer.

Cabbage Stuffed with Fish

Healthful cabbage is usually stuffed with meats, but I really like this stunning treatment when the leaves are filled with a fish puree and then napped in a red pepper sauce.

Yield: 6 servings | **Active time:** 25 minutes | **Start to finish:** 40 minutes

12 large leaves Savoy or green cabbage

1½ pounds white-fleshed fish fillet, skinned if necessary

2 tablespoons Asian sesame oil *

3 scallions, white parts and 2 inches of green tops, rinsed, trimmed, and chopped

2 garlic cloves, peeled and minced

1 tablespoon plus 1½ teaspoons lemon juice

1 tablespoon reduced-sodium soy sauce

1½ cups Seafood Stock (see recipe on page 42), purchased stock, or bottled clam juice

2 jarred roasted red peppers, rinsed and seeded, if necessary

1 tablespoon grated fresh ginger

Salt and freshly ground black pepper to taste

1. Bring a large pot of water to a boil. Add cabbage leaves and cook for 2 minutes, or until leaves are pliable. Drain and set aside.

2. Rinse fish, and pat dry with paper towels. Cut fish into ½-inch cubes. Puree ⅔ of fish in a food processor fitted with the steel blade or in a blender. Scrape mixture into a mixing bowl, and add remaining fish cubes. Set aside.

3. Heat sesame oil in a small skillet over medium heat. Add scallions and garlic and cook, stirring frequently, for 3 minutes, or until scallions are translucent. Add to fish along with 1 tablespoon lemon juice and soy sauce.

4. Lay out 2 cabbage leaves so they overlap slightly and divide fish mixture in the centers of leaves. Roll cabbage, tucking in the sides to enclose filling, and secure rolls with toothpicks. Place rolls in a bamboo steamer, and steam over boiling water for 10 minutes.

5. While rolls steam, combine stock, peppers, 1½ teaspoons lemon juice, ginger, salt, and pepper in a blender or food processor fitted with the steel blade; puree until smooth. Pour sauce into a small saucepan

* Available in the Asian aisle of most supermarkets and in specialty markets.

and bring to a boil over medium heat. Reduce sauce by ½, stirring frequently. To serve, place a pool of sauce on each plate, and top with a cabbage roll.

Note: The rolls can be prepared for steaming and the sauce can be made up to 1 day in advance and refrigerated, tightly covered. Add 5 minutes to the steaming time if chilled.

Each serving contains:
190 calories
59 calories from fat
7 g fat
1 g saturated fat
24 g protein
9 g carbohydrates

Variation:
- Substitute ground chicken or ground turkey for the fish. Steam for 15 minutes, or until an instant-read thermometer registers 165°F when inserted in the center of each roll.

Skinning fish is an easy task. Use an 8-inch chef's knife and start at one end of the fillet by pulling the skin away from the fillet with your fingers. Then hold on to the skin and push the knife away from you. It will scrape the fish away from the skin so the skin can then be discarded.

Fish in White Wine Sauce with Oranges

Like most fish dishes, this one is on the table quickly, and the combination of the sweet orange with herbs and tomatoes makes it especially attractive. Serve it with a tossed salad and some whole-wheat pasta.

Yield: 6 servings | **Active time:** 20 minutes | **Start to finish:** 35 minutes

2 tablespoons olive oil

3 scallions, white parts and 2 inches of green tops, rinsed, trimmed, and thinly sliced

1 celery rib, rinsed, trimmed, and sliced

3 garlic cloves, peeled and minced

1 (16-ounce) package frozen pearl onions, thawed

1 (14.5-ounce) can diced tomatoes, drained

¼ cup chopped fresh parsley

1½ cups Seafood Stock (recipe on page 42), Vegetable Stock (recipe on page 44), or purchased stock

½ cup dry white wine

1 cup orange juice

1 bay leaf

1½ pounds thick white-fleshed fish fillets, cut into 6 pieces, and rinsed

2 navel oranges, rind and white pith removed, and cut into ½-inch cubes

1 (10-ounce) package frozen cut green beans, thawed

Salt and freshly ground black pepper to taste

1. Heat olive oil in a large skillet over medium heat. Add scallions, celery, and garlic, and cook, stirring frequently, for 3 minutes, or until scallions are translucent. Add pearl onions, tomatoes, parsley, stock, white wine, orange juice, and bay leaf to the skillet. Bring to a boil, and simmer, uncovered, for 3 minutes.

2. Add fish and orange pieces to the skillet. Cover, bring to a boil, reduce the heat to low, and cook for 5 minutes. Turn fish gently with a slotted spatula, add green beans, and cook for an additional 5 minutes. Season to taste with salt and pepper. To serve, place fish on plates and surround each portion with vegetables and fruit. Serve immediately.

Note: The dish can be cooked up to 1 day in advance and refrigerated, tightly covered. Reheat it, covered, over low heat.

Each serving contains:
232 calories
50 calories from fat
5.5 g fat
1 g saturated fat
25 g protein
19 g carbohydrates

Variation:
- Substitute boneless, skinless chicken breast halves, pounded to an even thickness of ½ inch, for the fish. Cook chicken for 10–12 minutes, or until cooked through and no longer pink.

The white pith covering the flesh of all citrus fruits is very bitter, which is why you're told to remove it. While peeling is not an optional activity, if you're pressed for time, you can leave the pith on.

Sicilian Fish

The combination of salty capers with sweet, dried fruit and tomatoes is one of the defining aspects of Sicilian cuisine. If you want to dress the fish up a bit more, sprinkle some toasted pine nuts on top.

Yield: 6 servings | **Active time:** 25 minutes | **Start to finish:** 40 minutes

2 tablespoons olive oil
1 large onion, peeled and diced
4 garlic cloves, peeled and minced
1 (8-ounce) can tomato sauce
1 (14.5-ounce) can diced tomatoes, undrained
$3/4$ cup dry white wine
3 tablespoons chopped fresh parsley
2 teaspoons dried oregano
$1/2$ teaspoon dried thyme
2 bay leaves
$1/2$ cup raisins
$1/4$ cup capers, drained and rinsed
$1 1/4$ pounds thick white-fleshed fish fillet, rinsed and cut into 1-inch cubes
Salt and freshly ground black pepper to taste

1. Heat oil in a deep skillet over medium-high heat, swirling to coat the pan. Add onion and garlic, and cook, stirring frequently, for 3 minutes, or until onion is translucent. Stir in tomato sauce, tomatoes, wine, parsley, oregano, thyme, bay leaves, raisins, and capers. Bring to a boil, stirring occasionally.

2. Reduce the heat to low and simmer sauce, uncovered, for 15 minutes. Remove and discard bay leaves.

3. Add fish to sauce. Bring to a boil, cover pan, and simmer for 3 minutes. Turn off the heat, do not uncover the pan, and allow fish to sit for 5 minutes to complete cooking. Season to taste with salt and pepper, and serve immediately.

Note: The dish can be prepared up to 1 day in advance and refrigerated, tightly covered. Reheat it, covered, over low heat, stirring occasionally.

Each serving contains:
217 calories
52 calories from fat
6 g fat
1 g saturated fat
20 g protein
17 g carbohydrates

Variations:
- Substitute 1 pound of boneless, skinless chicken breast, cut into $^3/_4$-inch cubes, for the fish. Cook chicken for 5–7 minutes, or until cooked through and no longer pink.
- Substitute dried currants or chopped dried apricots for the raisins.

Mexican Fish with Olives

Most of Mexico borders either the Gulf of Mexico or the Pacific Ocean, so it is not surprising that there are countless delicious fish dishes as part of the cuisine. I like this one because the chile and smoked Spanish paprika give the sauce great depth of flavor.

Yield: 6 servings | **Active time:** 20 minutes | **Start to finish:** 35 minutes

2 tablespoons olive oil

2 medium onions, peeled and thinly sliced

4 garlic cloves, peeled and minced

1 jalapeño or serrano chile, seeds and ribs removed, and finely chopped

1 tablespoon chili powder

1 tablespoon smoked Spanish paprika

2 teaspoons dried oregano

1 (14.5-ounce) can diced tomatoes, undrained

1½ cups Seafood Stock (recipe on page 42) or purchased stock

2 tablespoons lemon juice

2 tablespoons tomato paste

½ cup sliced pimiento-stuffed green olives

1¼ pounds thick white-fleshed fish fillets, rinsed and cut into serving pieces

Salt and freshly ground black pepper to taste

1. Heat oil in a large skillet over medium-high heat, swirling to coat the pan. Add onion, garlic, and chile. Cook, stirring frequently, for 3 minutes, or until onions are translucent. Stir in chili powder, paprika, and oregano. Cook for 1 minute, stirring constantly.

2. Add tomatoes, stock, lemon juice, and tomato paste. Stir well. Bring to a boil, reduce the heat to low, and simmer sauce, uncovered, for 15–20 minutes, or until vegetables are tender.

3. Add olives and fish to the skillet, spooning vegetables and sauce on top of fillets. Cover the skillet, and cook fish for 5 minutes. Turn fillets gently with a slotted spatula and cook for an additional 3–5 minutes, or until fish flakes easily. Season to taste with salt and pepper, and serve immediately.

Note: The dish can be prepared up to 1 day in advance and refrigerated, tightly covered. Reheat it over low heat, covered, until hot.

Each serving contains:

194 calories

74 calories from fat

8 g fat

1 g saturated fat

21 g protein

46 g carbohydrates

Variation:

- Substitute 6 boneless, skinless chicken thighs for the fish, omit the lemon juice, and substitute chicken stock for the seafood stock. Add chicken to the skillet when the sauce starts simmering, and cook chicken until it is cooked through and no longer pink.

It's rare that a recipe specifies more than a few tablespoons of tomato paste, which is why it always ends up drying out in the refrigerator. Instead, line an ice cube tray with plastic wrap, and freeze 1 tablespoon portions of the remaining tomato paste.

Fish with Onions and Potatoes

The combination of potatoes and onions is called hash browns in the United States, but in classic French cooking those dishes are dubbed *Lyonnaise,* from the city of Lyon. The crispy vegetables topped by the moist, flavorful fish are really a winner.

Yield: 6 servings | **Active time:** 20 minutes | **Start to finish:** 55 minutes

2 tablespoons olive oil

1 pound large redskin potatoes, scrubbed and cut into ½-inch dice

2 large sweet onions (such as Vidalia or Bermuda), peeled and cut into ½-inch dice

3 garlic cloves, peeled and minced

1 teaspoon dried thyme

Salt and freshly ground black pepper to taste

1½ pounds thick white-fleshed fish fillets, rinsed and cut into serving pieces

1 teaspoon herbes de Provence

1. Preheat the oven to 500°F, and place a baking sheet in the oven as it preheats. Pour oil onto the baking sheet, and swirl to coat the pan. Add potatoes, onion, garlic, and thyme. Toss to coat well with oil. Bake for 25 minutes, turning occasionally with a spatula, or until potatoes and onions are browned. Season to taste with salt and pepper.

2. Sprinkle fish with salt and pepper, and rub with herbes de Provence. Place fish on top of vegetables, and bake for 10 minutes per inch of thickness, or until cooked but still slightly translucent in the center.

3. Remove the pan from the oven, and serve immediately.

Note: The vegetables can be cooked up to 6 hours in advance and kept at room temperature. Reheat them in the oven before baking the fish.

Each serving contains:

203 calories

44 calories from fat

5 g fat

1 g saturated fat

23 g protein

16 g carbohydrates

Variation:

- Add ½ cup crumbled cooked bacon to the vegetables at the same time the fish is added.

Fish continues to cook after it leaves a heat source, so to avoid overcooking it's best to stop baking or grilling fish when there's still a little translucency in the center of the piece. By the time it's plated and served it will become opaque.

Creole Fish on Spinach

Thin fish fillets are topped with a savory stuffing made with the "Holy Trinity" of Creole cooking—celery, bell pepper, and scallions. The fish is nestled on a bed of lightly creamed spinach, and the dish is your whole meal.

Yield: 6 servings | **Active time:** 20 minutes | **Start to finish:** 35 minutes

- 2 tablespoons unsalted butter
- 2 celery ribs, rinsed, trimmed, and chopped
- 1/2 green bell pepper, seeds and ribs removed, and chopped
- 6 scallions, white parts and 3 inches of green tops, rinsed, trimmed, and chopped
- 3 garlic cloves, peeled and minced
- 1/2 cup Seafood Stock (recipe on page 42), purchased stock, or bottled clam juice
- 2 tablespoons chopped fresh parsley
- 1/2 teaspoon dried thyme
- Cajun seasoning to taste
- 3/4 cup plain breadcrumbs
- Salt and freshly ground black pepper to taste
- 2 (10-ounce) packages frozen leaf spinach, thawed
- 1/3 cup half-and-half
- 1 1/2 pounds thin white-fleshed fish fillets
- Vegetable oil spray

1. Preheat the oven to 400°F, and grease a 9 x 13-inch baking pan with vegetable oil spray.
2. Heat butter in a skillet over medium heat. Add celery, green bell pepper, scallions, and garlic. Cook, stirring frequently, for 3 minutes, or until scallions are translucent. Stir in stock, parsley, thyme, and Cajun seasoning. Remove the pan from the stove, and stir in breadcrumbs. Season to taste with salt and pepper, and set aside.
3. Place spinach in a colander and press with the back of a spoon to extract as much liquid as possible. Place spinach in the prepared pan, and stir in half-and-half. Season to taste with salt and pepper, and spread spinach out evenly.
4. Divide stuffing between fillets, and place them on top of spinach. Bake for 15–20 minutes, or until fish is opaque and stuffing is lightly brown. Serve immediately.

Note: The fish can be prepared for baking up to 1 day in advance and refrigerated, tightly covered. If chilled, begin by baking fish, covered with foil, for 10 minutes. Then uncover the pan, and bake for an additional 10–15 minutes.

Each serving contains:
245 calories
69 calories from fat
8 g fat
4 g saturated fat
27 g protein
15 g carbohydrates

Variation:
- For an Italian-inspired dish, substitute Italian breadcrumbs for the plain, omit the Cajun seasoning, and add ¼ cup freshly grated Parmesan cheese to the stuffing. Season stuffing to taste with salt and pepper.

Herb-Crusted Fish

I usually make a double batch of this recipe, because it is delicious cold for lunch the next day, or I scrape off the topping and transform the leftover fish into a salad with chopped vegetables. It's an incredibly fast and easy recipe, and one that always pleases people who say they "don't like fish."

Yield: 6 servings | **Active time:** 10 minutes | **Start to finish:** 25 minutes

1½ pounds thick white-fleshed fish fillets, cut into serving pieces
Salt and freshly ground black pepper to taste
½ cup Italian breadcrumbs
2 teaspoons butter, melted
¼ cup chopped fresh parsley
¼ cup freshly grated Parmesan cheese
1 teaspoon dried thyme

1. Preheat the oven to 425°F, and line a 9 x 13-inch baking dish with aluminum foil. Rinse fish and pat dry with paper towels. Sprinkle fish with salt and pepper, and place fillets into the baking pan.
2. Combine breadcrumbs, butter, parsley, Parmesan cheese, and thyme in a small bowl. Pat topping onto fish.
3. Bake fish for 10–12 minutes, or until cooked through but still slightly translucent in the center. Allow fish to rest for 5 minutes, then serve immediately.

Note: The topping can be prepared up to 1 day in advance and refrigerated, tightly covered.

Each serving contains:
154 calories
32 calories from fat
4 g fat
2 g saturated fat
23 g protein
59.5 g carbohydrates

Variation:
- Substitute 1 pound boneless pork loin, trimmed of all fat and cut into 6 slices, for the fish.

Crispy "Fried" Fish

In the same way that you can enjoy the texture of fried chicken without the fat, you can also enjoy crispy fish. This easy beer batter, made with whole-wheat flour, is seasoned with spicy Cajun seasoning, and dinner is on the table in minutes.

Yield: 6 servings | **Active time:** 10 minutes | **Start to finish:** 20 minutes

$^1/_4$ cup whole-wheat flour

3 tablespoons all-purpose flour

Cajun seasoning to taste

$^2/_3$ cup lager beer

$1^1/_4$ pounds thin white-fleshed fish fillets

2 tablespoons vegetable oil, divided

1. Preheat the oven to 300°F, and line a baking sheet with aluminum foil.
2. Combine whole-wheat flour, all-purpose flour, and Cajun seasoning in a medium bowl. Whisk in beer to create a batter.
3. Rinse fish, and pat dry with paper towels. Heat 1 tablespoon oil in a large skillet over medium-high heat, swirling to coat the pan.
4. Coat $^1/_2$ of fish fillets with batter, allowing excess to drip back into the mixing bowl. Add fish to the pan, and cook for 2–3 minutes per side, or until crispy, turning fish gently with a slotted spatula. Remove fish from the pan, drain on paper towels, and keep warm in the oven while frying remaining fish in remaining oil in the same manner. Serve immediately.

Note: The batter can be prepared up to 4 hours in advance and kept at room temperature. Fry fish just prior to serving.

Each serving contains:

148 calories

46 calories from fat

5 g fat

1 g saturated fat

18.5 g protein

5 g carbohydrates

Variations:

- Substitute 2 tablespoons chili powder and salt and pepper to taste for the Cajun seasoning.
- Substitute 1 tablespoon Italian seasoning and salt and pepper to taste for the Cajun seasoning.

Spanish Baked Fish with White Beans

Both the fish and the beans absorb flavor from the white wine and tomatoes with which they're baked. Smoked Spanish paprika gives the dish some heartiness without making it spicy.

Yield: 6 servings | **Active time:** 15 minutes | **Start to finish:** 30 minutes

1¼ pounds thick white-fleshed fish fillets, cut into serving pieces
1 tablespoon olive oil
1 small onion, peeled and chopped
3 garlic cloves, peeled and minced
2 tablespoons smoked Spanish paprika
1 teaspoon dried thyme
1 (15-ounce) can cannellini beans, drained and rinsed
1 (14.5-ounce) can diced tomatoes, undrained
½ cup dry white wine
2 tablespoons chopped fresh parsley
Salt and freshly ground black pepper to taste
Vegetable oil spray

1. Preheat the oven to 425°F, and lightly grease a 9 x 13-inch baking dish with vegetable oil spray. Rinse fish, and pat dry with paper towels. Arrange fish in the prepared dish.
2. Heat oil in a deep skillet over medium-high heat, swirling to coat the pan. Add onion and garlic, and cook, stirring frequently, for 3 minutes, or until onion is translucent. Stir in paprika and thyme, and cook for 1 minute, stirring constantly.
3. Add beans, tomatoes, wine, and parsley to the skillet, and bring to a boil, stirring occasionally. Reduce the heat to medium, and simmer sauce 3 minutes. Pour sauce over fish.
4. Cover the baking dish with foil, and bake fish for 15–20 minutes, or until fish is cooked through and flakes easily. Season to taste with salt and pepper, and serve immediately.

Note: The dish can be prepared up to 1 day in advance and refrigerated, tightly covered. Reheat it, covered, in a 350°F oven for 20–25 minutes, or until hot.

Each serving contains:
230 calories
35 calories from fat
4 g fat
1 g saturated fat
24 g protein
22 g carbohydrates

Variation:
- Substitute 1 pound boneless, skinless chicken breast halves, cut into serving pieces, for the fish. Cook for 20–25 minutes, or until chicken is cooked through and no longer pink.

Smoked Spanish paprika is one of my favorite ingredients; it adds such great flavor to foods without any fat! The pimiento peppers are smoked over an oak fire, and the resulting powder gives foods an intoxicating aroma and nuance of smoky flavor.

Seafood Sausages

The food processor reinvented cooking for almost everyone I know; mine has a dedicated corner in the dishwasher because I use it daily. With the food processor you can make this pureed fish mixture quickly. Then poach it into sausage shapes and top it with a tomato sauce.

Yield: 6 servings | **Active time:** 20 minutes | **Start to finish:** 45 minutes

> 1½ pounds white-fleshed fish fillet, cut into 1-inch pieces
> 2 large egg whites
> ¼ cup half-and-half
> 2 tablespoons chopped fresh parsley
> 1 teaspoon herbes de Provence
> ½ pound salmon fillet, skinned, and finely chopped
> Salt and freshly ground black pepper to taste
> 1½ cups Herbed Tomato Sauce (recipe on page 38) or purchased
>   marinara sauce, heated
> Vegetable oil spray

1. Bring a large pot of water to a boil. Cut 12 (1-foot-square) pieces of aluminum foil. Set aside.
2. Combine fish, egg whites, half-and-half, parsley, and herbes de Provence in a food processor fitted with the steel blade. Puree until smooth, and scrape mixture into a mixing bowl. Stir salmon into the mixture, and season to taste with salt and pepper.
3. Lightly grease one side of each foil square with vegetable oil spray. Place a spoonful of the sausage mixture on one side and form with your fingers into a cylinder. Roll the foil, twisting the ends to seal the package tightly. Repeat until all sausages are formed.
4 Add sausage packages to the boiling water, and regulate the heat so that they are just simmering. Cover the pot, and simmer the sausages for 15 minutes.
5. Remove sausages from water with tongs, and allow them to rest for 10 minutes. Gently unwrap sausages over the sink, allowing any water that has seeped in to drain. Serve immediately, topped with tomato sauce.

Note: The sausages can be prepared up to 1 day in advance and refrigerated, tightly covered. Reheat them, covered, in a 325°F oven for 10–12 minutes, or until hot.

Each serving contains:
271 calories
98 calories from fat
11 g fat
3 g saturated fat
31 g protein
10 g carbohydrates

Variation:
- Substitute any finely chopped fish or shellfish—such as scallops or shrimp—for the salmon. It's nice to have the other fish be of a contrasting color.

Fish Florentine

Here's a key to reading menus: When you see something described as "Florentine," there's spinach involved somehow. In this case, a creamy spinach topping goes on top of the fish fillets, and low-fat ricotta cheese is a wonderful complement to the fish.

Yield: 6 servings | **Active time:** 20 minutes | **Start to finish:** 35 minutes

> 6 (5–6-ounce) thick white-fleshed fish fillets
> Salt and freshly ground black pepper to taste
> 2 (10-ounce) packages frozen leaf spinach, thawed
> 1 tablespoon olive oil
> 1 small onion, peeled and finely chopped
> 3 garlic cloves, peeled and minced
> 2 tablespoons chopped fresh parsley
> 1 teaspoon dried thyme
> ³/₄ cup low-fat ricotta cheese
> Vegetable oil spray

1. Preheat the oven to 375°F, and grease a 9 x 13-inch baking pan with vegetable oil spray. Rinse fish, and pat dry with paper towels. Sprinkle fish with salt and pepper, and set aside. Place spinach in a colander, and press with the back of a spoon to extract as much liquid as possible. Set aside.

2. Heat oil in a skillet over medium-high heat. Add onion and garlic, and cook, stirring frequently, for 3 minutes, or until onion is translucent. Add spinach, parsley, and thyme, and cook for an additional 2 minutes, stirring frequently. Remove the skillet from the heat, and stir in ricotta. Season to taste with salt and pepper.

3. Arrange fish in the prepared pan, and top each portion with ¹/₆ of spinach mixture. Bake fish for 15–18 minutes, or until fish is cooked through and flakes easily. Serve immediately.

Note: The fish can be prepared for baking up to 6 hours in advance and refrigerated, tightly covered. Add 5 minutes to the baking time if spinach mixture is chilled.

Each serving contains:

246 calories

55 calories from fat

6 g fat

2 g saturated fat

40 g protein

9 g carbohydrates

Variation:

- Substitute boneless, skinless chicken breasts, pounded to an even thickness of $1/2$ inch between 2 sheets of plastic wrap, for the fish. Bake for 20 minutes, or until chicken is cooked through and no longer pink.

A great trick for low-calorie cooking is placing the garnish ingredients on top of food as it bakes to keep it moist without fat. Traditional fish Florentine is baked on the spinach and topped with lots of melted butter; this version delivers all the same flavors with a fraction of the fat.

Fish Jambalaya

Jambalaya, from the bayous of Louisiana, is the first cousin to Spanish paella, on which it was based. It's really a one-pot dish of vegetables, rice, and fish, and it can be personalized in countless ways.

Yield: 6 servings | **Active time:** 20 minutes | **Start to finish:** 40 minutes

2 tablespoons olive oil

1 large onion, peeled and diced

3 garlic cloves, peeled and minced

1 green bell pepper, seeds and ribs removed, and diced

2 celery ribs, rinsed, trimmed, and sliced

1 cup long-grain white rice

2 tablespoons paprika

2 teaspoons dried oregano

1 teaspoon dried thyme

1¾ cups Chicken Stock (recipe on page 40) or purchased stock

1 (14.5-ounce) can diced tomatoes, drained

1 bay leaf

1 pound thick white-fleshed fish fillets, rinsed and cut into 1-inch cubes

¾ cup frozen peas, thawed

Salt and freshly ground black pepper to taste

1. Heat oil in a deep, covered skillet over medium-high heat. Add onion, garlic, green bell pepper, celery, and rice. Cook, stirring frequently, for 3 minutes, or until onion is translucent. Add paprika, oregano, and thyme, and cook for 1 minute, stirring constantly.

2. Stir stock, tomatoes, and bay leaf into the skillet, and bring to a boil over medium-high heat. Cover the skillet, reduce the heat to low, and cook for 15 minutes, or until rice is almost tender. Stir in fish and peas, and cook for 5–7 minutes, or until fish is cooked through, and rice is tender and has absorbed all of liquid.

3. Remove and discard bay leaf, season to taste with salt and pepper, and serve immediately.

Note: The dish can be prepared up to 2 days in advance and refrigerated, tightly covered. Reheat it, covered, in a 350°F oven for 20–25 minutes, or until hot.

Each serving contains:
290 calories
56 calories from fat
6 g fat
1 g saturated fat
20.5 g protein
38 g carbohydrates

Variations:
- Substitute 1 pound of boneless, skinless chicken, cut into ³/₄-inch cubes, for the fish. Add it to the skillet along with the liquids.
- Substitute a combination of baked ham and turkey sausage for the fish.

Fish Provençale

This dish, hailing from the sun-drenched province in southern France, is similar to a ratatouille topped with fish. The vegetable mélange contains eggplant, onion, garlic, and zucchini cooked in a tomato sauce. Enjoy it with some whole-wheat couscous or brown rice.

Yield: 6 servings | **Active time:** 25 minutes | **Start to finish:** 35 minutes

1 (1-pound) eggplant, cut into ¾-inch dice
Salt
3 tablespoons olive oil, divided
1 large onion, peeled and diced
3 garlic cloves, peeled and minced
2 small zucchini, rinsed, trimmed, and sliced
1 (14.5-ounce) can diced tomatoes, undrained
1 (8-ounce) can tomato sauce
3 tablespoons chopped fresh parsley
2 teaspoons herbes de Provence
Freshly ground black pepper to taste
1½ pounds thick white-fleshed fish fillet, rinsed and cut into serving pieces
¼ cup freshly grated Parmesan cheese
Vegetable oil spray

1. Place eggplant in a colander, and sprinkle cubes liberally with salt. Place a plate on top of eggplant cubes, and weight the plate with some cans. Place the colander in the sink or on a plate, and allow eggplant to drain for 30 minutes. Rinse eggplant cubes, and squeeze hard to remove water. Wring out remaining water with a cloth tea towel.

2. Preheat the oven to 400°F, and grease a 9 x 13-inch baking dish with vegetable oil spray.

3. While eggplant sits, heat 1 tablespoon oil in a large skillet over medium-high heat, swirling to coat the pan. Add onion, garlic, and zucchini, and cook, stirring frequently, for 3 minutes, or until onion is translucent. Scrape mixture into a mixing bowl, and set aside.

4. Return skillet to the stove, and add remaining oil, swirling to coat the pan. Add eggplant cubes, and cook over medium-high heat, stirring frequently, for 5 minutes, or until eggplant softens. Return onion mixture to the skillet, and add tomatoes, tomato sauce, parsley, and

herbes de Provence. Bring to a boil, and simmer mixture over medium heat, uncovered, for 10 minutes, or until vegetables are soft. Season to taste with salt and pepper, and scrape mixture into the prepared baking dish.

5. Arrange fish on top of vegetables, and sprinkle fish with salt, pepper, and Parmesan cheese. Bake fish for 10–15 minutes, or until cooked through and flesh flakes easily. Serve immediately.

Note: The vegetable mixture can be made up to 2 days in advance and refrigerated, tightly covered. Reheat it over low heat until simmering before baking the fish.

Each serving contains:
224 calories
75 calories from fat
8 g fat
2 g saturated fat
25.5 g protein
13 g carbohydrates

Variation:
- Substitute 6 boneless, skinless chicken thighs for the fish, and bake them at 375°F for 30–40 minutes, or until cooked through and no longer pink.

Grilled Caribbean Fish

Heady rum, fruit juices, and herbs flavor the marinade for this easy grilled fish. It does need time to marinate, but putting the dish together can be accomplished at record speed. Try some sautéed bananas or plantains with it.

Yield: 6 servings | **Active time:** 15 minutes | **Start to finish:** 2½ hours, including 2 hours to marinate

> 1½ pounds thick firm-fleshed white fish fillet, cut into serving pieces
> ½ small onion, peeled and chopped
> 2 garlic cloves, peeled and minced
> ½ cup orange juice
> ½ cup dry white wine
> 2 tablespoons rum
> 2 tablespoons lime juice
> 2 tablespoons reduced-sodium soy sauce
> 2 tablespoons chopped fresh parsley
> 2 teaspoons dried rosemary, crumbled
> Salt and freshly ground black pepper to taste
> 2 tablespoons olive oil

1. Rinse fish, and pat dry with paper towels. Combine onion, garlic, orange juice, wine, rum, lime juice, soy sauce, parsley, rosemary, salt, and pepper in a heavy resealable plastic bag, and mix well. Add oil, and mix well again.

2. Add fish to marinade, and marinate for a minimum of 2 hours, and up to 8 hours, refrigerated, turning the bag occasionally.

3. Light a charcoal or gas grill, or preheat the oven broiler. Remove fish from marinade, reserving marinade. Grill or broil fish for 3–4 minutes per side, depending on thickness, turning fillets gently with a spatula.

4. While fish grills, boil down marinade until it is reduced by ½. Spoon a few tablespoons over each portion of fish. Serve immediately.

Note: The fish can be served either hot or at room temperature.

Each serving contains:

175 calories

30 calories from fat

3 g fat

1 g saturated fat

22 g protein

11 g carbohydrates

Variation:

- Substitute 1¼ pounds boneless pork loin, trimmed of all fat, for the fish. Grill pork for 4–5 minutes per side, or until cooked through.

One of the first rules of food safety is never to reuse a marinade that has been in contact with raw poultry, meat, or seafood–unless it has been boiled as in this recipe. Simmer the marinade for at least 2 minutes, or reduce it as directed in a recipe. While you may think that nothing could be wrong if the food was refrigerated while it marinates, the marinade could have absorbed bacteria from the food.

Tuna Melt with Olives

A tuna melt is like a cross between a grilled cheese sandwich and a tuna salad sandwich, and in this case tomatoes and kalamata olives enliven the dish even more.

Yield: 6 servings | **Active time:** 10 minutes | **Start to finish:** 15 minutes

6 slices whole-wheat bread

3 (6-ounce) cans water-packed light tuna, drained

2 celery ribs, rinsed, trimmed, and chopped

1 shallot, peeled and chopped

1/3 cup chopped kalamata olives

2 tablespoons chopped fresh parsley

2 tablespoons lemon juice

3 tablespoons reduced-fat mayonnaise

Salt and freshly ground black pepper to taste

3 ripe plum tomatoes, rinsed, cored, seeded, and thinly sliced

3/4 cup grated sharp cheddar cheese

1. Preheat the oven broiler, and line a baking sheet with aluminum foil. Toast bread in a toaster, and set aside.
2. Combine tuna, celery, shallot, olives, parsley, lemon juice, and mayonnaise in a mixing bowl. Stir well, and season to taste with salt and pepper.
3. Place bread on the prepared baking sheet, and divide tuna mixture on top of each slice, smoothing it evenly with a spatula. Top tuna with tomato slices, and then sprinkle with cheese.
4. Broil sandwiches 6 inches from the broiler element for 2–4 minutes, or until cheese is bubbling and golden brown. Serve immediately.

Note: The tuna salad can be made up to 1 day in advance and refrigerated, tightly covered. Do not broil the sandwiches until just prior to serving.

Each serving contains:

266 calories

86 calories from fat

9.5 g fat

4 g saturated fat

29 g protein

15 g carbohydrates

Free-Style Tuna Salad Niçoise

Classic *Salade Niçoise* is fussy to make because it calls for a meticulous and labor-intensive presentation. This recipe achieves the same blending of flavors, colors, and textures in merely minutes.

Yield: 6 servings | **Active time:** 15 minutes | **Start to finish:** 30 minutes

> 2 large redskin potatoes, scrubbed and cut into $3/4$-inch dice
> 3 large eggs
> $1/2$ pound green beans, rinsed, trimmed, and cut into 1-inch lengths
> 3 ripe plum tomatoes, rinsed, cored, seeded, and diced
> 3 tablespoons capers, drained and rinsed
> 3 (6-ounce) cans water-packed light tuna, drained
> $2/3$ cup Rosemary Vinaigrette (recipe on page 27) or Balsamic Vinaigrette (recipe on page 26)
> 6 cups bite-sized pieces romaine or iceberg lettuce, rinsed and dried
> Salt and freshly ground black pepper to taste

1. Bring a large pot of salted water to a boil. Add potatoes and eggs and boil for 10–12 minutes, or until potatoes are almost tender. Add green beans, and cook for 2 minutes. Remove eggs from the pot with a slotted spoon, and cover eggs with cold water. Drain potatoes and green beans, and plunge into ice water to stop the cooking action. Drain, and place in a mixing bowl. Peel eggs, and cut each into quarters. Add to the mixing bowl.

2. Add tomatoes, capers, and tuna to the mixing bowl. Toss gently with $1/2$ of dressing. Toss lettuce with remaining dressing, and divide lettuce between six plates or mound on a platter. Top with salad, season to taste with salt and pepper, and serve immediately.

Note: The salad mixture can be prepared up to 1 day in advance and refrigerated, tightly covered. Do not add the dressing until just prior to serving.

Each serving contains:

243 calories
54 calories from fat
6 g fat
1 g saturated fat
28 g protein
19 g carbohydrates

Low-Cal Tuna Noodle Casserole

As promised earlier in this book, here's an updated version of your child-hood favorite made without a can of cream of mushroom soup, and fit-ting the definition of low-calorie. If you want to splurge on calories, go ahead and crumble some potato chips on top.

Yield: 6 servings | **Active time:** 20 minutes | **Start to finish:** 45 minutes

6 ounces medium egg noodles
2 tablespoons unsalted butter, divided
1 large onion, peeled and diced
2 celery ribs, rinsed, trimmed, and diced
1/2 pound mushrooms, wiped with a damp paper towel, trimmed, and diced
3 (6-ounce) cans water-packed light tuna, undrained
3 tablespoons all-purpose flour
1 cup skim milk
2 tablespoons chopped fresh parsley
1/2 teaspoon dried thyme
Salt and freshly ground black pepper to taste
Vegetable oil spray

1. Preheat the oven to 375°F, and grease a 2-quart casserole with veg-etable oil spray. Bring a large pot of salted water to a boil over high heat. Add noodles, and cook according to package directions until tender. Drain, and place noodles in the prepared casserole.
2. Melt 1 tablespoon butter in a skillet over medium heat, swirling to coat the pan. Add onion, celery, and mushrooms and cook, stirring frequently, for 5–7 minutes, or until onion is translucent. Add tuna, and cook for an additional 5–7 minutes, or until vegetables are soft. Scrape mixture into the casserole.
3. While vegetables cook, heat remaining butter in a small saucepan over low heat. Add flour, and cook for 2 minutes, stirring constantly. Whisk in milk, and bring to a boil over medium heat. Add parsley and thyme, and simmer for 2 minutes. Add sauce to casserole, season to taste with salt and pepper, and stir well.
4. Bake for 25–30 minutes, or until bubbly. Serve immediately.

Note: The dish can be prepared for baking up to 1 day in advance and refrigerated, tightly covered. Cover with foil and bake for 10 minutes, then uncover and bake for 25–30 minutes.

Each serving contains:

258 calories

58 calories from fat

6 g fat

3 g saturated fat

27 g protein

22 g carbohydrates

Variation:

- Substitute 2 cups finely diced cooked chicken for the tuna, and add ½ cup chicken stock to the skillet along with the chicken.

As long as a casserole is made with foods that are entirely cooked, it's better to get them ready to bake in advance and then add some minutes to their time in the oven rather than bake and reheat them; it keeps them from drying out. This cannot be done, however, with casseroles containing raw protein like chicken. Those must be thoroughly cooked or they could lead to foodborne illness.

Tuna and Garbanzo Bean Salad

I adore the nutty flavor and meaty texture of garbanzo beans, and they pair very well with tuna in this filling salad napped with one of my low-calorie vinaigrette dressings.

Yield: 6 servings | **Active time:** 15 minutes | **Start to finish:** 25 minutes

1 (15-ounce) can garbanzo beans, drained and rinsed

$^2/_3$ cup Rosemary Vinaigrette (recipe on page 27), divided

2 large cucumbers, peeled, halved, seeded, and diced

3 ripe plum tomatoes, rinsed, cored, seeded, and diced

$^1/_4$ cup chopped fresh parsley

3 (6-ounce) cans water-packed light tuna, drained

6 cups bite-sized pieces iceberg or romaine lettuce, rinsed and dried

1. Place garbanzo beans in a mixing bowl, and add $^1/_2$ of dressing, cucumbers, tomatoes, parsley, and tuna. Allow mixture to sit for 10 minutes.
2. Toss lettuce with remaining dressing, and divide onto six plates or place on a platter. Top with salad, and serve immediately.

Note: The salad can be prepared up to 6 hours in advance and refrigerated, tightly covered. Do not toss lettuce with dressing until just prior to serving.

Each serving contains:
219 calories
38 calories from fat
4 g fat
1 g saturated fat
23 g protein
22 g carbohydrates

Variation:
- Substitute 2 cups diced cooked chicken for the tuna.

Chapter 8:
Vibrant and Vegetarian Entrees

You probably knew this was coming—recipes for vegetarian dishes. After all, this is a book on low-calorie cooking, right? But wait. Don't draw any speedy conclusions about pages of dishes that you can term "bunny food." How about a big plate of pasta with a sauce made from sweet caramelized onions, or a mélange of vegetables similar to a ratatouille but topped with eggs? A stuffed baked potato for lunch? Why not?

Those are the recipes you'll find in this chapter, but what you won't find are salads of any type. My assumption is that anyone following a low-calorie diet probably has a library of salad recipes. Instead, I developed for you a group of hearty and vibrantly flavored vegetable dishes using a wide range of seasonings and types of vegetables.

Keeping in mind that we're talking about low-cost food as well as low-cal food, you won't find such extravagances as stuffed artichokes or wild mushroom stew. But you will find recipes drawn from around the world, united only by their use of vegetables.

TERRIFIC TOFU

No wonder they call it a wonder food! Lately, researchers are discovering more and more nutritional benefits of soy products. For example, soybeans are the only known plant source of complete protein, for adults although not for children.

Complete protein is the term used for a food that contains all the essential amino acids in the appropriate proportions that are part of the growth and maintenance of cells. Meats and some dairy products have complete protein, while grains and beans contain incomplete proteins. Blending two incomplete proteins, such as rice and beans, can produce complete protein. But in the plant world, soy alone has it all.

In addition, the Food and Drug Administration (FDA) has approved a health claim stating that diets containing 25 grams of soy protein a day may reduce the risk of heart disease.

While soy milk is growing in popularity as an alternative to cow's milk, the way we eat soybeans most often is as tofu. A custard-like substance, it is also called bean curd, which is the literal translation from

Chinese. Tofu has very little innate flavor of its own, so it absorbs the flavor of the sauce in which it's cooked.

Making tofu is similar to making cheese. Both methods involve curds and whey. For tofu, the first step is to create soy milk by soaking, grinding, boiling, and straining dried soybeans. Either salts or acids are then added to the soy milk to cause coagulation. Then the curds are extracted from the whey, and packaged. The texture of the tofu depends on the amount of water pressed out. Here are the three consistencies you'll find in the supermarket:

- **Soft (or silken) tofu.** This tofu has had no water removed, and it has the texture of a silky custard. While it's great added to smoothies or juices, it does not hold together when cooked.

- **Firm tofu.** Some whey has been pressed out, so this tofu has the texture of raw meat, although that texture will not change once it's cooked. It bounces back when pressed with your finger, and it can easily be picked up by chopsticks or a fork.

- **Dry (also called extra-firm) tofu.** The most solid of all tofu, it has the texture of cooked meat and crumbles easily. It's this type of tofu that's used in processed tofu products.

What's confusing when looking at tofu packages is that the net weights vary although the package size is uniform, because the net weight is that of the product with the weight of the surrounding water subtracted from the total. Silken tofu packages weigh 1 pound, while the net weight of firm tofu can vary between 12 and 14 ounces, depending on the brand. Dry tofu can have a net weight as low as 8 ounces.

While tofu is a vegetable product, it is as perishable as delicate seafood, so make sure you look for the "sell by" date before buying it. Tofu is packed in water, and the water should be changed daily once it's home. It will last up to a week with fresh water daily, but may spoil within a few days otherwise. Tofu can be frozen for up to three months. The texture will change to become slightly chewy after it's thawed.

You'll notice that these recipes specify light tofu, which is relatively new to the market. It is a reduced calorie product, but I can discern no difference in the flavor or texture. A portion of firm tofu has about 70 calories, while there are only 40 calories in the light version.

Spicy Glazed Tofu

The slices of tofu are coated with a spice mixture and then fried to give them a crispy exterior. Serve this dish with steamed vegetables or stewed beans.

Yield: 4 servings | **Active time:** 5 minutes | **Start to finish:** 15 minutes

2 tablespoons chili powder
1½ teaspoons ground cumin
1½ teaspoons dried oregano
Salt and freshly ground black pepper to taste
¼ cup boiling water
3 tablespoons pure maple syrup
2 tablespoons lemon juice
1 (14-ounce) package light firm tofu
1 tablespoon vegetable oil

1. Combine chili powder, cumin, oregano, salt, and pepper in a small bowl. Combine boiling water, maple syrup, and lemon juice in a small cup. Drain tofu, pat dry with paper towels, and cut into 8 slices. Rub spice mixture on both sides of slices.
2. Heat oil in a large skillet over medium-high heat, swirling to coat the pan. Add tofu, and cook for 4–5 minutes, or until brown and crusty. Turn slices gently with a slotted spatula, and cook the remaining side for 4–5 minutes. Add liquid to the pan, and shake the pan to coat slices. Serve immediately.

Note: The tofu can be prepared for frying up to 1 day in advance and refrigerated, tightly covered.

Each serving contains:
122 calories
38 calories from fat
4 g fat
1 g saturated fat
8 g protein
14 g carbohydrates

Variation:
- For a less spicy dish, substitute paprika for the chili powder, and substitute 2 teaspoons Italian seasoning for the ground cumin and oregano.

Curried Tofu

This is a delightful way to enjoy both tofu and crisp-tender vegetables. The spices in the curry powder are balanced by the creamy richness of the coconut milk. Serve this dish over brown rice.

Yield: 6 servings | **Active time:** 15 minutes | **Start to finish:** 25 minutes

>   2 (14-ounce) packages light firm tofu
>   2 tablespoons vegetable oil
>   1 large onion, peeled and sliced
>   2 large carrots, peeled and grated
>   3 garlic cloves, peeled and minced
>   3–4 tablespoons curry powder
>   1 teaspoon ground cumin
>   1 cup light coconut milk
>   2 cups broccoli florets
>   2 cups cauliflower florets
>   ⅓ cup raisins
>   Salt and freshly ground black pepper to taste

1. Drain tofu, cut into ¾-inch dice, and set aside. Heat oil in a medium saucepan over medium heat, swirling to coat the pan. Add onion, carrot, and garlic. Cook, stirring frequently, for 5 minutes, or until onion is soft. Stir in curry powder and cumin. Cook, stirring constantly, for 1 minute.

2. Add coconut milk, raise the heat to medium-high, and bring to a boil. Add broccoli, cauliflower, tofu, and raisins, and reduce the heat to medium-low. Simmer, uncovered, for 5–7 minutes, or until vegetables are crisp-tender. Season to taste with salt and pepper. Serve immediately.

Note: The dish can be prepared up to 1 day in advance and refrigerated, tightly covered. Reheat it, covered, over low heat, stirring gently occasionally.

Each serving contains:
189 calories
76 calories from fat
8.5 g fat
3 g saturated fat
12 g protein
17 g carbohydrates

Variation:

- Boneless chicken breast, cut into ½-inch cubes, can be substituted for the tofu and will cook for the same length of time. Make sure that the chicken is cooked through and no longer pink.

Always buy curry powder in small jars, because its life is only about 2 months, rather than the 6 months of many other spices. This ground blend, made up of up to 20 herbs and spices, loses its flavor and aroma very quickly.

Spicy Chinese Tofu on Cabbage

This is similar to a salad, because the crunchy cabbage is raw. But the tofu is cooked in a spicy broth with mushrooms, which wilts the cabbage when the mixture is added to the bowl.

Yield: 4 servings | **Active time:** 25 minutes | **Start to finish:** 40 minutes

1/4 cup reduced-sodium soy sauce

3 tablespoons rice vinegar

1 teaspoon wasabi powder *

2 garlic cloves, peeled and minced

1 (14-ounce) package light firm tofu, drained and cut into 1-inch cubes

2 tablespoons Asian sesame oil *

1/2 pound mushrooms, wiped with a damp paper towel, trimmed, and sliced

4 cups shredded Napa cabbage

1 large carrot, peeled and shredded

4 scallions, white parts and 3 inches of green tops, rinsed, trimmed, and sliced

Salt and freshly ground black pepper to taste

1. Combine soy sauce, vinegar, wasabi powder, and garlic in a heavy resealable plastic bag. Add tofu, and marinate for 10 minutes, turning the bag occasionally.

2. Heat oil in a large skillet over medium-high heat, swirling to coat the pan. Add mushrooms, and cook for 3 minutes, stirring frequently. Add tofu and marinade, and cook for an additional 3 minutes, or until mushrooms soften.

3. Combine cabbage, carrot, and scallions in a mixing bowl, and pour hot tofu mixture on top. Toss to coat vegetables with dressing, season to taste with salt and pepper, and serve immediately.

Note: The tofu mixture can be made 1 day in advance and refrigerated, tightly covered. Reheat it over low heat, stirring occasionally.

* Available in the Asian aisle of most supermarkets and in specialty markets.

Each serving contains:

154 calories

63 calories from fat

7 g fat

1 g saturated fat

12 g protein

12 g carbohydrates

Variation:

- For a non-spicy dish, omit the wasabi and add 2 tablespoons hoisin sauce to the marinade.

You don't have a better diet friend than cabbage; there's a little more than 200 calories in a 2-pound head! It's great and crunchy cold, or it's wonderfully silky cooked. And it's always at the low end of the price chart in any supermarket!

Southwestern Black Bean Cakes

These cakes, made from ground canned beans mixed with spices and chiles, are as meaty as any hamburger you could eat. They're delicious with a tossed salad and a side order of Mexican rice.

Yield: 6 servings | **Active time:** 20 minutes | **Start to finish:** 20 minutes

    3 tablespoons olive oil, divided
    1 medium onion, peeled and coarsely chopped
    3 garlic cloves, peeled and minced
    2 jalapeño or serrano chiles, seeds and ribs removed, and diced
    2 tablespoons chili powder
    1½ tablespoons ground cumin
    2 (15-ounce) cans black beans, drained and rinsed
    ½ cup chopped fresh cilantro
    ½ cup water
    Salt and cayenne to taste
    1 cup tomato salsa (optional)

1. Heat 1 tablespoon oil in a large skillet over medium-high heat, swirling to coat the pan. Add onion, garlic, and chiles, and cook, stirring frequently, for 3 minutes, or until onion is translucent. Add chili powder and cumin, and cook, stirring constantly, for 1 minute. Add black beans, cilantro, and water. Bring to a boil and simmer mixture, stirring frequently, for 3 minutes.
2. Transfer mixture to a food processor fitted with the steel blade and puree. Scrape mixture into a mixing bowl, and season to taste with salt and cayenne. Divide mixture into 12 parts, and form each into a patty ¼ inch thick.
3. Heat remaining oil in a heavy, large skillet over high heat, swirling to coat the pan. Add bean cakes, and cook for 1–2 minutes per side, or until crisp, turning gently with a slotted spatula. Drain cakes on paper towels, and continue until all cakes are cooked.
4. To serve, place cakes on a plate, and top each with tomato salsa, if using. Serve immediately.

Note: The bean mixture can be made up to 1 day in advance and refrigerated, tightly covered. Fry cakes just prior to serving.

Each serving contains:

191 calories

62 calories from fat

7 g fat

1 g saturated fat

7 g protein

22.5 g carbohydrates

Variation:

- Substitute kidney beans for the black beans, and substitute 2 chipotle chiles in adobo sauce for the fresh chiles.

It's a chile pepper's seeds and ribs that contain almost all of the capsaicin, the chemical compound that delivers the pepper's punch. Since small chiles have proportionately more seeds and ribs to flesh, a general rule is the smaller the chile, the hotter the pepper.

Chinese Spicy Eggplant

You've probably seen this dish on many menus in Chinese restaurants, and it's both spicy and hearty. Serve it over brown rice accompanied by some Chinese pickles for low-cal crunch.

Yield: 6 servings | **Active time:** 20 minutes | **Start to finish:** 30 minutes

3 (1-pound) eggplants
$1^{1}/_{2}$ cups Vegetable Stock (recipe on page 44) or purchased stock
3 tablespoons dry sherry
3 tablespoons reduced-sodium soy sauce
2 tablespoons Chinese chile paste with garlic *
1 tablespoon cider vinegar
$1^{1}/_{2}$ teaspoons granulated sugar
2 tablespoons Asian sesame oil *
4 garlic cloves, peeled and minced
3 tablespoons grated fresh ginger
6 scallions, white parts and 3 inches of green tops, rinsed, trimmed, and chopped
Salt and freshly ground black pepper to taste

1. Rinse eggplants, discard stem ends, and cut into $^{3}/_{4}$-inch dice. Combine stock, sherry, soy sauce, chile paste, vinegar, and sugar in a mixing bowl. Stir well, and set aside.
2. Heat oil in a wok or frying pan over high heat, swirling to coat the pan. When oil is very hot but not quite smoking, add eggplant. Cook, stirring constantly, for 2–3 minutes, or until lightly browned
3. Add garlic, ginger, and scallions, and stir-fry 1 minute. Stir sauce, and add to the pan. Cook, stirring constantly, for 3 minutes. Reduce the heat to low, cover the pan, and simmer for 10–12 minutes, or until eggplant is tender. Season to taste with salt and pepper, and serve immediately.

Note: The dish can be prepared up to 6 hours in advance and kept at room temperature.

* Available in the Asian aisle of most supermarkets and in specialty markets.

Each serving contains:

131 calories

46 calories from fat

5 g fat

1 g saturated fat

4 g protein

19 g carbohydrates

Variation:

- To make this a heartier dish, cook ½ pound finely diced boneless pork loin along with the eggplant.

Peel a small section of the large piece of ginger. Grate the peeled portion, using the rest of the ginger as a handle to keep your fingers safely away from the grater. The ginger also remains fresh longer if it's not peeled, so there's a second advantage.

Asian Ratatouille with Baked Eggs

Ratatouille, long before the movie, was known as a classic French vege-table dish. This version has Asian seasonings, and it's topped with eggs for more protein. This is also a wonderful side dish for 10–12 people if made without the eggs, and as a side dish it can be served hot, at room temperature, or chilled.

Yield: 6 servings | **Active time:** 20 minutes | **Start to finish:** 45 minutes

1 cup Vegetable Stock (recipe on page 44) or purchased stock
1 (8-ounce) can tomato sauce
¼ cup dry sherry
3 tablespoons black bean sauce *
3 tablespoons hoisin sauce *
3 tablespoons reduced-sodium soy sauce
3 tablespoons red wine vinegar
1 teaspoon Chinese chile paste with garlic *
2 tablespoons Asian sesame oil *
1 large onion, peeled and diced
3 garlic cloves, peeled and minced
3 tablespoons grated fresh ginger
3 small zucchini, rinsed, trimmed and cut into ½-inch slices
3 small yellow squash, rinsed, trimmed and cut into ½-inch slices
½ pound mushrooms, wiped with a damp paper towel, and halved
    if small or quartered if large
1 (1-pound) eggplant, rinsed, trimmed, and cut into ½-inch dice
Salt and freshly ground black pepper to taste
6 large eggs
Vegetable oil spray

1. Preheat the oven to 375°F, and grease a 9 x 13-inch baking dish with vegetable oil spray. Combine stock, tomato sauce, sherry, black bean sauce, hoisin sauce, soy sauce, vinegar, and chile paste in a small bowl, and stir well.

2. Heat oil in a deep skillet over medium-high heat, swirling to coat the pan. Add onion, garlic, and ginger, and cook, stirring frequently, for 3 minutes, or until onion is translucent. Add zucchini, yellow squash, mushrooms, and eggplant. Cook, stirring frequently, for 3 minutes, or until squash begins to soften.

* Available in the Asian aisle of most supermarkets and in specialty markets.

3. Add sauce mixture, and bring to a boil, stirring occasionally. Cover the skillet, reduce the heat to low, and cook for 10 minutes. Uncover the skillet, increase the heat to medium, and simmer for 5 minutes, stirring frequently, or until vegetables are tender and sauce has thickened slightly. Season to taste with salt and pepper.

4. Scrape vegetables into the prepared pan. Smooth top of vegetable mixture, and then create 6 indentations. Break 1 egg into each indentation, and sprinkle with salt and pepper.

5. Bake eggs for 10–12 minutes, or to desired doneness. Serve immediately.

Note: The vegetable mixture can be prepared up to 2 days in advance and refrigerated, tightly covered. Reheat it over low heat, covered, until simmering before baking with eggs.

Each serving contains:
228 calories
95 calories from fat
11 g fat
2 g saturated fat
13 g protein
22 g carbohydrates

Zucchini is Italian in origin, and its native name was retained when it was integrated into American cooking. Choose small zucchini because they tend to have a sweeter flavor and the seeds are tender and less pronounced.

Stir-Fried Sesame Vegetables

Here's a light and colorful dish of crispy Chinese-style vegetables made with aromatic sesame oil and topped with crunchy sesame seeds. Like all Asian food, it goes best with brown rice.

Yield: 6 servings | **Active time:** 25 minutes | **Start to finish:** 25 minutes

2 tablespoons sesame seeds

1 cup Vegetable Stock (recipe on page 44) or purchased stock

1/4 cup reduced-sodium soy sauce

3 tablespoons dry sherry

2 tablespoons Asian sesame oil *

3 garlic cloves, peeled and minced

5 scallions, white parts and 4 inches of green tops, rinsed, trimmed, and sliced

3 tablespoons grated fresh ginger

1 (1-pound) head Napa cabbage, rinsed, trimmed, and sliced into 1/2-inch pieces on the diagonal

1 large green bell pepper, seeds and ribs removed, and thinly sliced

1/2 pound mushrooms, wiped with a damp paper towel, trimmed, and thinly sliced

1 tablespoon cornstarch

2 tablespoons cold water

Salt and freshly ground black pepper to taste

1. Place sesame seeds in a small, dry skillet over medium heat. Toast seeds for 2 minutes, or until browned, shaking the pan frequently. Set aside. Combine vegetable stock, soy sauce, and dry sherry in a small bowl. Stir well, and set aside.

2. Heat oil in a wok or large skillet over medium-high heat, swirling to coat the pan. Add garlic, scallions, and ginger. Cook, stirring constantly, for 30 seconds, or until fragrant. Add cabbage, green bell pepper, and mushrooms. Cook, stirring constantly, for 1 minute.

3. Add liquid mixture to the skillet, raise the heat to high, and cook for 2 minutes, or until vegetables are crisp-tender. Mix cornstarch and water in a small cup, and add to the wok. Cook for 1 minute, or until slightly thickened. Season to taste with salt and pepper. Serve immediately, sprinkling sesame seeds on each serving.

* Available in the Asian aisle of most supermarkets and in specialty markets.

Note: The vegetables can be prepped up to 6 hours in advance and refrigerated, tightly covered.

Each serving contains:

158 calories

99 calories from fat

11 g fat

2 g saturated fat

4 g protein

11 g carbohydrates

Variation:

- For a non-vegetarian dish, add $3/4$ pound boneless, skinless chicken breast, cut into $1/2$-inch dice, with the vegetables. Cook chicken until it is cooked through and no longer pink.

Here's a way to minimize the number of bowls you'll have to wash after cooking a stir-fried dish: Layer the vegetables, starting with the one added last at the bottom of the bowl, and separate the layers with plastic wrap. When it's time to add the next ingredient, just reach in, grab the sheet of plastic wrap, and toss the vegetables in.

Spinach and Carrot Loaf

This pureed vegetable terrine is extremely easy to make and very elegant to serve. It's subtly seasoned, so what you taste is the pure flavor of the vegetables. Their vivid orange and green colors create a dramatic presentation.

Yield: 6 servings | **Active time:** 25 minutes | **Start to finish:** 1³/₄ hours

> 1 pound carrots, peeled and sliced
> 1 pound frozen chopped spinach, thawed
> 1 tablespoon unsalted butter
> 1 large onion, peeled and finely chopped
> 1 large egg
> 5 large egg whites
> 2 tablespoons freshly grated Parmesan cheese
> Salt and freshly ground black pepper to taste
> Vegetable oil spray

1. Preheat the oven to 350°F, grease the inside of a 9 x 5-inch loaf pan with vegetable oil spray, line the bottom of the loaf pan with parchment paper or waxed paper, and grease the paper. Bring a large kettle of water to a boil over high heat.

2. Steam carrots in a vegetable steamer for 10–15 minutes, or until tender. Allow carrots to cool for 10 minutes. Place spinach in a colander, and press with the back of a spoon to extract as much liquid as possible.

3. Melt butter in a medium skillet over medium heat, swirling to coat the pan. Add onion, and cook, stirring frequently, for 7 minutes, or until onion is soft. Allow to cool slightly. Beat egg with egg whites lightly, and divide mixture equally into 2 mixing bowls.

4. Place carrots, along with ½ of onion, ½ of egg, ½ of Parmesan cheese, salt, and pepper in a food processor fitted with the steel blade or in a blender. Puree until smooth, and scrape puree into the loaf pan, smoothing the top with a spatula. Repeat with the spinach, using the remaining ingredients.

5. Smooth the top and place the loaf pan in a 9 x 13-inch baking pan. Pour boiling water halfway up the sides of the loaf pan and bake for 1 hour. Remove from the oven and allow to stand for 20 minutes in the water before unmolding. Serve hot, at room temperature, or chilled.

Note: The loaf can be made to the point of baking up to 1 day in advance; allow it to reach room temperature before baking. Or, it can be totally cooked up to 3 days in advance, and served cold.

Each serving contains:
110 calories
34 calories from fat
4 g fat
2 g saturated fat
9 g protein
13 g carbohydrates

Variations:
- Substitute parsnips or cauliflower for the carrots.
- Substitute chopped broccoli, cooked according to package directions, for the spinach.

Spinach Soufflé

I hesitated to include this recipe, because a friend ate it at my house and said "I'm afraid of soufflés!" But there's really no need to be, and this dish is very low in calories, as are all vegetable soufflés. The only trick is to make sure your mixing bowl is totally free of grease; to do that, wipe the inside with a paper towel moistened with vinegar.

Yield: 6 servings | **Active time:** 20 minutes | **Start to finish:** 55 minutes

⅓ cup plain breadcrumbs
1 (10-ounce) package frozen chopped spinach, thawed
1 tablespoon unsalted butter
2 tablespoons all-purpose flour
½ cup skim milk
Salt and freshly ground black pepper to taste
3 tablespoons freshly grated Parmesan cheese
6 large egg whites, at room temperature
Vegetable oil spray

1. Preheat the oven to 400°F. Grease the inside of a 6-cup soufflé dish with vegetable oil spray, and coat the interior with breadcrumbs, shaking over the sink to remove any excess. Place spinach in a colander, and push with the back of a spoon to extract as much liquid as possible. Set aside.

2. Melt butter in a small saucepan over low heat. Add flour and cook over low heat, stirring constantly, for 2 minutes. Whisk in milk, salt, pepper, and cheese and bring to a boil, whisking constantly, until thick. Stir in spinach, and set aside.

3. Place egg whites in a totally grease-free bowl, and beat at medium speed with an electric mixer until frothy. Increase the speed to high and beat until stiff peaks form. Gently fold spinach mixture into egg whites, and scrape into the prepared soufflé dish.

4. Place soufflé in the center of the oven, and immediately reduce the temperature to 375°F. Bake for 35–45 minutes, until soufflé has puffed and top is brown; the baking time depends on whether you like soufflés wet or dry in the center. Serve immediately.

Note: The spinach mixture can be prepared up to 4 hours in advance and kept at room temperature. Do not beat the egg whites or bake the soufflé until just prior to serving.

Each serving contains:

100 calories

31 calories from fat

3.5 g fat

2 g saturated fat

8 g protein

10 g carbohydrates

Variation:

- Substitute frozen chopped broccoli, cooked according to package directions and pureed, for the spinach.

Here's an easy way to separate eggs: Start by washing your hands with hot water and soap. Then you can break the egg, and pour it into your slightly cupped hand. Let the white fall through your fingers into the bowl.

Broccoli-Stuffed Baked Potatoes

These creamy potatoes fool people. The orange tone leads you to think they're filled with cheddar cheese, and the flavor conveys all the richness of a potato moistened with sour cream and chives.

Yield: 6 servings | **Active time:** 15 minutes | **Start to finish:** 1½ hours

> 3 large Idaho baking potatoes
> ¾ cup Vegetable Stock (recipe on page 44) or purchased stock
> 1 small onion, peeled and finely chopped
> 2 garlic cloves, peeled and finely minced
> 1 (10-ounce) package frozen chopped broccoli, thawed
> 1½ teaspoons paprika
> Salt and freshly ground black pepper to taste
> 1 cup plain nonfat yogurt
> 4 scallions, white parts and 3 inches of green tops, rinsed,
>   trimmed, and chopped
> 3 tablespoons freshly grated Parmesan cheese

1. Preheat the oven to 400°F. Scrub potatoes with a stiff brush and prick them in several places with a meat fork. Bake in the center of the oven for 1 hour, or until tender when pierced with a knife.

2. While potatoes bake, combine stock, onion, and garlic in a small saucepan. Bring to a boil over medium heat, and simmer, uncovered, for 10 minutes, stirring occasionally. Cook broccoli according to package directions. Drain well, and set aside.

3. Remove potatoes from the oven and cut in half. Scrape pulp into a bowl, reserving shells. Add onion mixture, paprika, salt, pepper, yogurt, and scallions. Beat with an electric mixer until light and fluffy. Stir in broccoli.

4. Stuff potato mixture back into shells, and sprinkle with Parmesan cheese. Bake for an additional 10–15 minutes, or until hot and lightly browned. Serve immediately.

Note: Potatoes can be stuffed up to 2 days in advance and refrigerated, tightly covered. To cook straight from the refrigerator, preheat the oven to 375°F and bake for 20–25 minutes.

Each serving contains:

120 calories

9 calories from fat

1 g fat

0.5 g saturated fat

7 g protein

22 g carbohydrates

Variation:

- Substitute cauliflower for the broccoli.

Like many other healthful foods, it's what we do to potatoes that make them high in calories; it's not the basic food. Your average baking potato has just 110 calories and contains as much potassium as a banana and 45 percent of the daily value of vitamin C.

Caribbean Stuffed Eggplant

The filling is made up of the eggplant pulp seasoned with flavorful ingredients and eggs, which gives the dish the soft texture of a custard. You can serve it topped with Mexican Tomato Sauce (recipe on page 39), or just as is with a tossed salad.

Yield: 6 servings | **Active time:** 20 minutes | **Start to finish:** 55 minutes

3 (1-pound) eggplants

2 tablespoons olive oil, divided

6 scallions, white parts and 3 inches of green tops, rinsed, trimmed, and thinly sliced

2 garlic cloves, peeled and minced

1/3 cup plain breadcrumbs

1/4 cup skim milk

1 large egg, lightly beaten

2 large egg whites

2 tablespoons chopped fresh cilantro

1 teaspoon dried basil

1/4 teaspoon hot red pepper sauce, or to taste

Salt and freshly ground black pepper to taste

Vegetable oil spray

1. Preheat the oven to 375°F, line a 10 x 14-inch baking dish with aluminum foil, and grease the foil with vegetable oil spray.

2. Cut eggplants in half lengthwise, and trim off caps. Heat 1 tablespoon olive oil in large skillet over medium heat. Slash cut sides of eggplants several times, being careful not to cut through to the skin. Place eggplants cut side down in oil, cover, and cook 10 minutes. This may have to be done in batches.

3. Scoop out pulp using a grapefruit knife or a sharp spoon, leaving shells about 1/4 inch thick. Set shells aside. Coarsely chop eggplant pulp. Heat remaining oil in the skillet over medium heat, and add pulp, scallions, and garlic. Cook 5 minutes, stirring frequently. Allow to cool for 10 minutes.

4. In a large bowl, moisten breadcrumbs with milk and mix thoroughly with egg and egg whites. Stir in cooked pulp mixture, cilantro, basil, and hot pepper sauce. Season to taste with salt and pepper.

5. Stuff eggplant shells with mixture, and place them in the prepared pan. Cover the pan with aluminum foil, and bake for 20 minutes. Uncover the pan, and bake for an additional 15 minutes, or until a toothpick inserted in the center comes out clean. Serve immediately.

Note: The eggplants can be prepared for baking up to 1 day in advance and refrigerated, tightly covered. Add 15 minutes to initial baking time if chilled.

Each serving contains:
140 calories
50 calories from fat
6 g fat
1 g saturated fat
6 g protein
19 g carbohydrates

Variation:
- For a non-vegetarian dish, add 2 cups shredded cooked chicken to the cooked eggplant mixture.

Sweet and Hot Spaghetti Squash

The combination of sweet and hot—in this case from hot red pepper flakes and tasty hoisin sauce—enlivens the delicacy of the spaghetti squash. It really does look like a bowl of pasta when cooked.

Yield: 6 servings | **Active time:** 15 minutes | **Start to finish:** 1 1/4 hours

    1 (4-pound) spaghetti squash
    Salt and freshly ground black pepper to taste
    1 tablespoon Asian sesame oil *
    4 scallions, white parts and 4 inches of green tops, rinsed,
        trimmed, and chopped
    3 garlic cloves, peeled and minced
    2 tablespoons grated fresh ginger
    1/2–1 teaspoon crushed red pepper flakes, or to taste
    1 cup Vegetable Stock (recipe on page 44) or purchased stock
    3 tablespoons hoisin sauce *
    2 tablespoons reduced-sodium soy sauce
    2 teaspoons cornstarch
    2 tablespoons cold water

1. Preheat the oven to 350°F, and line a baking sheet with aluminum foil.
2. Cut squash in half lengthwise, and discard seeds. Sprinkle cut surfaces with salt and pepper. Place squash, cut sides down, on a baking sheet and roast until fork-tender, about 1 hour.
3. While squash bakes, heat oil in a small saucepan over medium-high heat. Add scallions, garlic, ginger, and red pepper flakes, and cook, stirring frequently, for 1 minute, or until fragrant. Add stock, hoisin sauce, and soy sauce, and cook over medium heat, stirring occasionally, for 5 minutes. Mix cornstarch and water in a small cup, and add to sauce. Cook for 2 minutes, or until slightly thickened. Set aside.
4. Remove squash from shell by combing halves lengthwise with the tines of a fork. To serve, place squash in a mixing bowl, and toss with sauce. Season to taste with salt and pepper, and serve immediately.

* Available in the Asian aisle of most supermarkets and in specialty markets.

Note: The dish can be prepared up to 2 days in advance and refrigerated, tightly covered. Reheat it, covered, in a 350°F oven for 20–25 minutes, or until hot.

Each serving contains:
149 calories
39 calories from fat
4 g fat
1 g saturated fat
3 g protein
28 g carbohydrates

Variation:
- Substitute 3 pounds yellow squash or zucchini for the spaghetti squash. Cut it into ½-inch slices, and steam over simmering water for 10–15 minutes, or until soft.

Spaghetti squash is a relative newcomer in the vegetable patch. Its popularity has grown because it can be sauced like spaghetti for those on low-carbohydrate or low-calorie diets. Shaped like a small watermelon, spaghetti squash weighs about 3–5 pounds, and once it is cooked and the flesh is forked vertically, it separates into distinct pasta-like strands.

Mexican Spaghetti Squash

Spaghetti squash is baked with tomatoes blended with Mexican spices, and then topped with creamy cheese in this dish. It can also serve as a side dish for 10–12 people and makes any simple entrée more elegant.

Yield: 6 servings | **Active time:** 15 minutes | **Start to finish:** 1³⁄₄ hours

1 (4-pound) spaghetti squash
Salt and freshly ground black pepper to taste
1 tablespoon olive oil
1 medium red onion, peeled and chopped
2 garlic cloves, peeled and minced
1 jalapeño or serrano chile, seeds and ribs removed, and finely chopped
2 teaspoons dried oregano
1 teaspoon ground cumin
1 (14.5-ounce) can diced tomatoes, undrained
1 (8-ounce) can tomato sauce
1 (4-ounce) can diced mild green chiles, drained
1 teaspoon granulated sugar
1 teaspoon cider vinegar
¹⁄₂ cup grated Monterey Jack cheese
¹⁄₄ cup chopped fresh cilantro
Vegetable oil spray

1. Preheat the oven to 350°F, and line a baking sheet with aluminum foil.
2. Cut squash in half lengthwise, and discard seeds. Sprinkle cut surfaces with salt and pepper. Place squash, cut sides down, on a baking sheet and roast until fork-tender, about 1 hour.
3. While squash bakes, heat oil in saucepan over medium-high heat. Add onion, garlic, and fresh chile, and cook, stirring frequently, for 3 minutes, or until onion is translucent. Add oregano and cumin, and cook, stirring constantly, for 1 minute. Add tomatoes, tomato sauce, canned chiles, sugar, vinegar, salt, and pepper to pan, and bring to a boil. Reduce the heat to low, and simmer for 20 minutes, stirring occasionally. Turn off the heat, and set aside.

4. Remove squash from shell by combing halves lengthwise with the tines of a fork. Place squash in prepared pan, and stir in sauce. Cover the pan with aluminum foil, and bake for 15 minutes. Remove foil, sprinkle with cheese and cilantro, and bake for an additional 15 minutes, or until cheese melts and top is lightly browned.

Note: The dish can be prepared up to 2 days in advance and refrigerated, tightly covered. Reheat it, covered, in a 350°F oven for 20–25 minutes, or until hot.

Each serving contains:
183 calories
63 calories from fat
7 g fat
2.5 g saturated fat
6 g protein
28 g carbohydrates

Variation:
- Substitute 3 pounds yellow squash or zucchini for the spaghetti squash. Cut it into ½-inch slices, and steam over simmering water for 10–15 minutes, or until soft.

Pasta Primavera

Primavera is the Italian word for "springtime," and although this dish sounds quintessentially Italian, it was born and bred in New York. Restaurateur Sirio Maccioni created it in the mid-1970s for his famed Le Cirque restaurant, and food writers popularized the dish nationally.

Yield: 6 servings | **Active time:** 20 minutes | **Start to finish:** 25 minutes

½ pound dried angel hair pasta, broken into 2-inch lengths
2 tablespoons olive oil
1 medium onion, peeled and chopped
3 garlic cloves, peeled and minced
3 small summer squash, rinsed, trimmed, and cut into ½-inch dice
¾ pound fresh mushrooms, wiped with a damp paper towel, trimmed, and thinly sliced
1 green bell pepper, seeds and ribs removed, and thinly sliced
1 (14.5-ounce) can diced tomatoes, drained
1½ cups Vegetable Stock (recipe on page 44) or purchased stock
¾ cup whole milk
3 tablespoons chopped fresh parsley
2 teaspoons Italian seasoning
1½ cups broccoli florets
½ cup frozen peas, thawed
Salt and crushed red pepper flakes to taste
½ cup freshly grated Parmesan cheese

1. Bring a large pot of salted water to a boil. Add pasta, and cook according to package directions until al dente. Drain, and keep warm.
2. While water heats, heat oil in a large skillet over medium-high heat, swirling to coat the pan. Add onion and garlic, and cook, stirring frequently, for 3 minutes, or until onion is translucent. Add squash, mushrooms, and green bell pepper. Cook for 3–5 minutes, or until mushrooms soften.
3. Add tomatoes, stock, milk, parsley, Italian seasoning, broccoli, and peas to the skillet. Bring to a boil over medium-high heat, and simmer, uncovered, for 3 minutes, stirring occasionally, or until vegetables are crisp-tender. Season to taste with salt and red pepper flakes, and simmer for an additional 2 minutes.
4. To serve, add drained pasta to skillet, and toss with cheese. Serve immediately.

Note: The dish can be completed up to the end of Step 3 up to 4 hours in advance, and kept at room temperature. Reheat it to a simmer before adding the pasta.

Each serving contains:
308 calories
78 calories from fat
9 g fat
2.5 g saturated fat
14 g protein
46 g carbohydrates

Variation:
- To make this a non-vegetarian dish, substitute chicken stock for the vegetable stock, and add $3/4$ pound boneless, skinless chicken breast, cut into $1/2$-inch cubes, to the skillet along with the squash and mushrooms. Cook until the chicken is cooked through and no longer pink.

Macaroni with White Beans, Tomatoes, and Sage

I'm on a campaign to promote sage; I love its musty aroma and slightly sharp flavor. In this fast and easy pasta dish it flavors the tomatoes and beans, and is balanced by heady Parmesan cheese.

Yield: 6 servings | **Active time:** 10 minutes | **Start to finish:** 25 minutes

½ pound whole-wheat macaroni or other small pasta
2 tablespoons olive oil
4 garlic cloves, peeled and minced
2 tablespoons dried sage
1 tablespoon chopped fresh parsley
1 (14.5-ounce) can petite diced tomatoes, undrained
1 (15-ounce) can cannellini beans, drained and rinsed
⅓ cup freshly grated Parmesan cheese
Salt and freshly ground black pepper to taste

1. Bring a large pot of salted water to a boil. Add pasta, and cook according to package directions until al dente. Drain pasta, and set aside.
2. While water heats, heat olive oil in a large skillet over medium-high heat. Add garlic, sage, and parsley and cook, stirring constantly, for 1 minute. Add tomatoes and beans, and simmer for 2 minutes.
3. Add pasta and Parmesan to the skillet, and season to taste with salt and pepper. Serve immediately.

Note: This pasta dish is also delicious served at room temperature or chilled as a salad.

Each serving contains:
294 calories
52 calories from fat
6 g fat
1.5 g saturated fat
13 g protein
48 g carbohydrates

Variation:
- This dish changes dramatically with the choice of herb. You can substitute basil, rosemary, or oregano for the sage.

Chapter 9:
(Almost) Guilt-Free Goodies

To many people it's not a meal unless it ends with dessert, and it certainly is not a party if there's nothing following the main course. The good news is that it's possible to eat desserts every day while staying on a low-calorie diet. Dessert, like every other course of a meal, runs the gamut from light and ethereal to heavy and hearty. What unites most of the recipes in this chapter is a reliance on the natural fructose of ripe fruit to sweeten a dessert.

And this chapter ends with some baked goods. Waking up to the aroma of muffins baking in the oven, or ending dinner with a sweet treat, is not inconsistent with maintaining a low-calorie lifestyle. But the amount of fat and refined sugar found in most baked goods and desserts needs to be judiciously controlled. In place of fat, these recipes rely on fruits and vegetables to deliver the same moisture to muffins and quick breads. And they lend their delicious flavors, too.

DEFINITION OF TERMS

As promised, the recipes in this book are consistent with the government's definition of low-calorie. But in this chapter there are a few exceptions. Some treats in the analysis are identified as "reduced-calorie." This means that they have at least 25 percent fewer calories than their "leaded" cousins. And the calorie counts prove this to be true.

The other exceptions are the two angel food cakes. They are just angel food cakes, which are inherently low in calories, and far more healthful than other types of baked goods. There is no low-calorie or reduced-calorie version of angel food cakes, and none is needed when you see how low they are naturally.

Cheesecake

As with many high-calorie foods, only a little cream cheese is needed to give this cake its richness. The light texture of the cheesecake and its citrus flavor make this a special dessert for any meal.

Yield: 6 servings | **Active time:** 20 minutes | **Start to finish:** 4 hours, including 3½ hours for chilling

    1 cup graham cracker crumbs
    1½ tablespoons unsalted butter, melted
    ½ teaspoon ground cinnamon
    1 tablespoon unflavored gelatin
    ½ cup skim milk
    2 ounces cream cheese, softened to room temperature
    ⅓ cup granulated sugar
    1¼ cups low-fat cottage cheese
    ½ cup plain nonfat yogurt
    ½ teaspoon pure vanilla extract
    2 tablespoons grated lemon zest
    3 large egg whites, at room temperature
    Pinch of cream of tartar

1. For crust, preheat the oven to 300°F. Combine crumbs, butter, and cinnamon, and press into the bottom and slightly up the sides of an 8-inch round cake pan. Bake in the center of the oven for 10 minutes. Remove crust from the oven, and set aside to cool.

2. For filling, sprinkle gelatin on top of skim milk to soften for 10 minutes. Place in a small saucepan and heat over medium heat, stirring constantly, until gelatin is dissolved and no granules remain. Set aside to cool.

3. In a mixing bowl, beat cream cheese with sugar until light and fluffy. Add cottage cheese, yogurt, vanilla, lemon zest, and gelatin mixture and beat until smooth. In a grease-free mixing bowl, beat egg whites at medium speed with an electric mixer until frothy. Add cream of tartar, raise the speed to high, and beat until stiff peaks form. Gently fold egg whites into cheese mixture, then pour into prepared crust and chill until set, at least 3½ hours.

Note: Cheesecake can be prepared up to 2 days in advance and refrigerated, tightly covered with plastic wrap.

Each reduced-calorie serving contains:

239 calories

76 calories from fat

8.5 g fat

4 g saturated fat

13 g protein

27 g carbohydrates

Variations:

- Substitute orange zest or lime zest for the lemon zest.
- Omit the lemon zest, and add 4 tablespoons of unsweetened cocoa powder.
- Substitute crushed gingersnap cookies or chocolate cookies for the graham cracker crumbs.

While it's more expensive, you use so little of it that it really makes a difference to use pure vanilla extract rather than artificial. The artificial extract gives foods a chemical flavor.

Citrus Angel Food Cake

The tangy tastes of orange and lemon are consistent with the light, airy quality of angel food cake. This cake can serve as the base for many mixed fruit salads, as well as being delicious by itself.

Yield: 8 servings | **Active time:** 25 minutes | **Start to finish:** 2½ hours

> ¾ cup orange juice
> 2 tablespoons finely grated orange zest
> 2 tablespoons finely grated lemon zest
> ¾ cup cake flour
> ⅛ teaspoon salt
> ¾ cup granulated sugar, divided
> 10 large egg whites, at room temperature
> 1 teaspoon cream of tartar

1. Preheat the oven to 350°F. Rinse a tube pan and shake it over the sink to remove excess moisture, but do not wipe it dry.
2. Combine orange juice, orange zest, and lemon zest in a small, heavy saucepan and bring to a boil over medium heat. Reduce by ¾, pour mixture into a soup bowl, and refrigerate until cool. Sift flour with salt and ¼ cup of sugar; set aside.
3. Place egg whites in a grease-free mixing bowl and beat at medium speed with an electric mixer until frothy. Add cream of tartar, raise the speed to high, and beat until soft peaks form. Add remaining sugar, 1 tablespoon at a time, and continue to beat until stiff peaks form and meringue is glossy. Lower the speed to low and beat in cooled orange juice mixture. Gently fold flour mixture into meringue and scrape batter into the tube pan.
4. Bake in the center of the oven for 45 minutes, then remove from the oven and invert cake in the pan onto a cake rack or the neck of a wine bottle for at least 1½ hours, or until cool. Run a knife or spatula around the outside of the pan to loosen cake and invert cake onto a serving plate.

Note: Cake can be prepared up to 1 day in advance, and kept at room temperature, tightly covered with plastic wrap after it has cooled and been inverted onto a serving plate.

Each serving contains:
146 calories
2 calories from fat
0 g fat
0 g saturated fat
6 g protein
31 g carbohydrates

Cream of tartar is an acidic ingredient that helps to stabilize egg whites so that they form a stiff meringue. You can substitute an equal amount of lemon juice, lime juice, or vinegar for cream of tartar to achieve the same result.

Chocolate Angel Food Cake

Angel food cakes are light and cholesterol-free desserts. This one is flavored with cocoa powder for the chocoholic of your acquaintance.

Yield: 8 servings | **Active time:** 20 minutes | **Start to finish:** 2½ hours

> 5 tablespoons unsweetened cocoa powder
> ¾ cup cake flour
> Pinch of salt
> ¾ cup granulated sugar, divided
> 10 large egg whites, at room temperature
> ¾ teaspoon cream of tartar
> 1 teaspoon pure vanilla extract

1. Preheat the oven to 350°F. Rinse out a tube pan and shake it over the sink, but do not wipe it dry. Set aside.
2. Sift together cocoa, flour, salt, and ¼ cup of sugar. Set aside.
3. Place egg whites in a grease-free bowl and beat at medium speed with an electric mixer until frothy. Add cream of tartar and continue beating, raising the speed to high, until soft peaks form. Continue beating, adding remaining sugar, 1 tablespoon at a time, until meringue forms stiff peaks and is shiny. With the mixer at the lowest speed, beat in vanilla. Gently fold cocoa mixture into egg whites, being careful to avoid streaks of white meringue. Scrape batter into the tube pan.
4. Bake in the center of the oven for 40–45 minutes Remove cake from the oven and invert the pan onto a rack or onto the neck of a wine bottle for at least 1½ hours, or until cool. Run a knife or spatula around the outside of the pan to loosen cake and invert cake onto a serving plate.

Note: Cake can be prepared up to 1 day in advance, and kept at room temperature, tightly covered with plastic wrap after it has cooled and been inverted onto a serving plate.

Each serving contains:
149 calories
5 calories from fat
1 g fat
0 g saturated fat
6 g protein
31 g carbohydrates

Variation:
- Dissolve 1 tablespoon instant espresso powder in 2 tablespoons boiling water, and beat it into batter along with the vanilla for a mocha cake.

Cocoa powder is made when chocolate liquor is pressed to remove ¾ of its cocoa butter. The remaining cocoa solids are processed to make fine unsweetened cocoa powder. It tastes very bitter and gives a deep chocolate flavor to baked goods.

Almond Meringue Cookies

These crispy almond-flavored meringues are very easy to make and an elegant treat for dessert or snacks.

Yield: 30 cookies | **Active time:** 15 minutes | **Start to finish:** 1½ hours

    3 large egg whites, at room temperature
    ½ teaspoon cream of tartar
    1 teaspoon almond extract
    ¾ cup granulated sugar
    ⅓ cup finely chopped almonds

1. Preheat the oven to 250°F. Line two cookie sheets with parchment paper or aluminum foil.
2. Place egg whites in a totally grease-free bowl, and beat at medium speed with an electric mixer until frothy. Add cream of tartar, raise the speed to high, and beat until soft peaks form. Beat in almond extract and then sugar, 1 tablespoon at a time. Continue to beat meringue until shiny and stiff. Gently fold in almonds and drop by tablespoons onto the baking sheets.
3. Bake in the center of the oven for 30 minutes, then turn the oven off and allow the meringues to sit in the oven, without opening the door, for another 30 minutes. Remove from the oven and allow meringues to cool on the baking sheets before removing.

Note: Meringues will remain fresh for more than a week in an airtight biscuit tin.

Each reduced-calorie 1-cookie serving contains:
27 calories
5 calories from fat
0.5 g fat
0 g saturated fat
1 g protein
5 g carbohydrates

Variations:

- Substitute pure vanilla extract and 3 tablespoons unsweetened cocoa powder for the almond extract and substitute miniature chocolate chips for the almonds.
- Substitute peppermint extract for the almond extract, and substitute crushed peppermint candy for the almonds.
- Substitute brown sugar for the granulated sugar, vanilla extract for the almond extract, and toasted pecans for the almonds.

An easy way to get eggs to room temperature is to cover the whole eggs in very hot tap water for 3 minutes. They will separate more easily, and the whites will be at the proper temperature for beating.

Rice Pudding

What could be a more soul-satisfying comfort food than creamy rice pudding? This version is flavored with tangy dried currants and a touch of orange from the marmalade and liqueur.

Yield: 6 servings | **Active time:** 15 minutes | **Start to finish:** 3 hours, including 2 hours for chilling

RICE

$\frac{1}{2}$ cup long-grain white rice

1 cup water

$1\frac{1}{2}$ cups skim milk

2 tablespoons granulated sugar

2 teaspoons unsalted butter

$\frac{1}{2}$ teaspoon pure vanilla extract

2 tablespoons dried currants

2 tablespoons fruit-only orange marmalade

1 tablespoon Triple Sec (optional)

PASTRY CREAM

3 tablespoons skim milk

2 teaspoons cornstarch

1 tablespoon granulated sugar

1 large egg

1. Bring rice and water to a boil over medium heat. Blanch rice for 5 minutes to remove some of the starch, drain, and return rice to the pan along with skim milk, sugar, butter, vanilla, currants, orange marmalade, and Triple Sec, if using. Bring to a boil over medium heat and reduce the heat to low. Cook rice, covered, for 30–40 minutes, stirring occasionally, or until rice is very tender and the mixture has thickened. Scrape rice into a mixing bowl.

2. Combine milk, cornstarch, and sugar in a small saucepan, and bring to a boil over low heat, stirring constantly and beating until thick and smooth. Remove the pan from the heat and whisk in egg. Stir pastry cream into rice and chill until cold, at least 2 hours.

Note: The rice pudding can be prepared up to 3 days in advance and refrigerated, tightly covered.

Each serving contains:

157 calories

20 calories from fat

2 g fat

1 g saturated fat

5 g protein

30 g carbohydrates

Variations:

- Substitute fruit-only blueberry jam and dried blueberries for the orange marmalade and dried currants.
- Substitute fruit-only apricot jam and chopped dried apricots for the orange marmalade and dried currants.
- Add 2 tablespoons unsweetened cocoa powder to the recipe.

Not all rice is created equal. Each of the thousands of species cooks at a different rate, and many require more or less liquid than others. So don't substitute rice, especially if it's a brown rice, which takes up to three times as long to cook as white rice.

Lemon Cheese Mousse

Eating this light mousse creates the same rich sensation as eating a lemon-scented cheesecake. Try topping it with some fresh blueberries or sliced strawberries when they're in season.

Yield: 6 servings | **Active time:** 15 minutes | **Start to finish:** 4¼ hours, including 4 hours for chilling

   1 tablespoon unflavored gelatin
   2 tablespoons cold water
   ¼ cup lemon juice
   8 ounces low-fat ricotta cheese
   1 large egg
   ¼ cup granulated sugar
   ¼ cup plain nonfat yogurt
   2 teaspoons grated lemon zest
   4 large egg whites
   ¼ teaspoon cream of tartar

1. Sprinkle gelatin over water to soften for 10 minutes in a small saucepan. Add lemon juice, and stir over low heat until gelatin is dissolved and no granules remain.
2. In a mixing bowl, beat ricotta with egg and sugar until light and fluffy. Beat in yogurt, lemon zest, and gelatin mixture and set aside.
3. Place egg whites in a grease-free mixing bowl and beat at medium speed with an electric mixer until frothy. Add cream of tartar, raise the speed to high, and beat until stiff peaks form.
4. Gently fold ricotta mixture into egg whites, and pour mousse into individual dishes or a serving bowl. Chill until set, about 4–6 hours.

Note: The mousse can be made up to 2 days in advance and refrigerated, tightly covered with plastic wrap.

Each serving contains:
105 calories
24 calories from fat
3 g fat
1 g saturated fat
9 g protein
12 g carbohydrates

Variation:
• Substitute lime juice for the lemon juice.

Mocha Mousse

Coffee and chocolate are an unbeatable combination. With this mousse, add the cinnamon if you want to replicate the flavor of cappuccino, the rich Italian breakfast drink.

Yield: 6 servings | **Active time:** 15 minutes | **Start to finish:** 3 hours, including 2½ hours for chilling

1 tablespoon unflavored gelatin
2 cups skim milk
¼ cup granulated sugar
1½ tablespoons instant espresso powder
3 tablespoons finely chopped bittersweet chocolate
¼ teaspoon ground cinnamon (optional)
5 large egg whites, at room temperature
Pinch of cream of tartar

1. In a small saucepan, sprinkle gelatin over skim milk to soften for 10 minutes. Stir in sugar, instant espresso, chocolate, and cinnamon, if using. Heat, stirring constantly, over medium-high heat until gelatin, coffee, and chocolate are dissolved and mixture is dark. Pour mixture into a mixing bowl and refrigerate until mixture is at least room temperature or slightly chilled. If mixture has begun to set, beat with a whisk until smooth.

2. Place egg whites in a grease-free mixing bowl and beat at medium speed with an electric mixer until frothy. Add cream of tartar, raise the speed to high, and beat until stiff peaks form.

3. Gently fold egg whites into mocha mixture and chill for at least 2½ hours, until mousse is set.

Note: The mousse can be prepared up to 2 days in advance and refrigerated, tightly covered with plastic wrap.

Each serving contains:
114 calories
26 calories from fat
3 g fat
2 g saturated fat
7 g protein
17 g carbohydrates

Bananas Baked with Rum

Breakfast at Brennan's in New Orleans—which may be where brunch was invented—frequently ends with Bananas Foster flambéed tableside. This is a healthier—not to mention safer—version of the dish.

Yield: 6 servings | **Active time:** 10 minutes | **Start to finish:** 25 minutes

> 6 medium ripe bananas
> 2 tablespoons lemon juice
> ¼ cup firmly packed dark brown sugar
> ¼ cup dark rum
> 1 tablespoon unsalted butter

1. Preheat oven to 350°F, and line a 9 x 13-inch baking pan with aluminum foil.
2. Peel and halve bananas lengthwise, and immediately roll in lemon juice to prevent discoloration. Arrange bananas in the baking pan.
3. Combine brown sugar, rum, and butter in a small saucepan and bring to a boil over medium heat. Simmer for 2 minutes, then pour syrup evenly over bananas. Bake in the center of the oven for 15 minutes, or until bananas are soft. Serve warm or at room temperature.

Note: The bananas can be prepared up to 2 days in advance and refrigerated, tightly covered with plastic wrap. Allow them to reach room temperature before serving.

Each serving contains:
165 calories
17 calories from fat
2 g fat
1 g saturated fat
1 g protein
35 g carbohydrates

Variation:
- Substitute granulated sugar and an orange-flavored liqueur such as Triple Sec or Cointreau for the brown sugar and rum.

Pear Clafoutis

A clafoutis (pronounced *kla-foo-tee*) is like a popover baked on top of fruit. The dessert comes from the Limosin region of France, and is a wonderful way to end brunch as well as dinner.

Yield: 8 servings | **Active time:** 10 minutes | **Start to finish:** 1 hour

> 2 large eggs
> 3 large egg whites
> ¼ cup granulated sugar
> ⅓ cup all-purpose flour
> 1 cup skim milk
> 2 tablespoons unsalted butter, melted
> 1 teaspoon pure vanilla extract
> 3 ripe pears, peeled, cored, and thinly sliced
> 2 tablespoons confectioners' sugar for dusting
> Vegetable oil spray

1. Preheat oven to 325°F, and grease a 9-inch-diameter, deep-dish pie plate or 9-inch-square pan with vegetable oil spray.
2. Combine eggs, egg whites, and sugar in a mixing bowl, and whisk well. Add flour, milk, butter, and vanilla, and whisk well again.
3. Arrange pears in the bottom of the prepared pan, and top with custard. Bake in the center of the oven for 50–60 minutes, or until set and golden brown. Remove the pan from the oven, and dust with confectioners' sugar. Serve immediately.

Note: The clafoutis can be prepared for baking up to 4 hours in advance and refrigerated, tightly covered. Do not bake it until just prior to serving.

Each serving contains:
147 calories
39 calories from fat
4 g fat
2 g saturated fat
5 g protein
23 g carbohydrates

Variation:
- Substitute 5 ripe plums for the pears.
- Substitute 2 cups pitted and halved sweet cherries for the pears.

Blueberry Grunt

A grunt is a colonial American dessert form; it's basically dumplings cooked on top of fruit.

Yield: 6 servings | **Active time:** 15 minutes | **Start to finish:** 30 minutes

2/3 cup orange juice

3 1/2 cups fresh or frozen blueberries

2 tablespoons fruit-only blueberry jam

1 tablespoon cornstarch

2 tablespoons cold water

3/4 cup all-purpose flour

1 tablespoon granulated sugar

1 teaspoon baking powder

Pinch of salt

3 tablespoons unsalted butter, cut into small pieces

1/3 cup skim milk

1/4 teaspoon pure vanilla extract

Vanilla frozen yogurt (optional)

1. Combine orange juice, blueberries, and jam in a large skillet with a lid. Bring to a boil over medium-high heat, stirring occasionally. Cover, reduce heat to medium, and simmer for 5 minutes, or until berries are cooked. Mix cornstarch into water, and stir to dissolve. Uncover the skillet, stir cornstarch mixture into fruit, and simmer for 2 minutes, or until slightly thickened.

2. Combine flour, sugar, baking powder, and salt. Cut in butter with a pastry blender, two knives, or your fingertips until the mixture resembles coarse meal. Add milk and vanilla to flour mixture, and mix just until moist dough forms. Spoon 6 mounds of dough on top of fruit.

3. Cover and simmer for 15 minutes, or until a toothpick inserted in dumplings comes out clean; do not uncover the pan while dumplings steam. Serve hot with vanilla frozen yogurt, if using.

Note: The fruit mixture can be made up to 1 day in advance and refrigerated, tightly covered. Reheat it to a simmer over low heat, stirring occasionally. Do not make the dumpling batter or cook the dumplings until just prior to serving.

Each serving contains:
195 calories
48 calories from fat
5 g fat
3 g saturated fat
3 g protein
35 g carbohydrates

Variations:
- Substitute peaches or a combination of berries for the blueberries. Cook until fruit is soft.
- Omit the vanilla, and add ½ teaspoon ground cinnamon to the dumpling batter.

While pastry blenders were a part of every cook's kitchen until a generation ago, they are now becoming rare, as fewer people make pie crust from scratch without the aid of a food processor. They look like a half-moon, with three or four wire blades attached to a handle. Rocking them back and forth through a bowl with flour and butter breaks up the butter into tiny pieces so the mixture resembles a coarse meal.

Strawberry Frozen Yogurt

Frozen yogurt can be a deceptive product; it promises health, but can be as high as ice cream in terms of calories. That's not true in this version; what you taste are the delicious fresh berries.

Yield: 6 servings | **Active time:** 5 minutes | **Start to finish:** Depends on ice cream freezer

1 pint strawberries, rinsed, hulled, and sliced if large
2 tablespoons crème de cassis or rum
3 tablespoons granulated sugar
1 pint plain nonfat yogurt
2 egg whites

Combine strawberries, crème de cassis, sugar, yogurt, and egg whites in a food processor fitted with the steel blade or in a blender. Puree until smooth. Freeze in an ice cream freezer according to manufacturer's instructions.

Note: Allow frozen yogurt to sit at room temperature for 20 minutes before serving if it's frozen very solid. The yogurt will keep for up to a week in the freezer.

Each serving contains:
101 calories
3 calories from fat
0 g fat
0 g saturated fat
6 g protein
16 g carbohydrates

Variation:
- Substitute raspberries, blueberries, or blackberries for the strawberries.

Maple Bourbon Frozen Yogurt

This is a wonderful winter dessert, when apples are clearly the most affordable fruit on the market. The subtle taste of maple is tantalizing as an accent.

Yield: 6 servings | **Active time:** 15 minutes | **Start to finish:** Depends on ice cream freezer

> 2 Red Delicious or McIntosh apples, peeled and grated
> 1/3 cup pure maple syrup
> 2 tablespoons water
> 1/4 teaspoon pure maple extract
> 2 tablespoons bourbon
> 2 cups plain nonfat yogurt
> 2 teaspoons lemon juice

1. Place apples in a small saucepan along with syrup, water, maple extract, and bourbon. Bring to a boil, and simmer over low heat, stirring occasionally, for 5–7 minutes, or until the apples are tender.
2. Place apple mixture in a food processor fitted with the steel blade or in a blender, and puree until smooth. Stir in yogurt and lemon juice, and freeze in an ice cream maker according to manufacturer's instructions.

Note: Allow frozen yogurt to sit at room temperature for 20 minutes before serving if it's frozen very solid. The yogurt will keep for up to a week in the freezer.

Each serving contains:
106 calories
2 calories from fat
0 g fat
0 g saturated fat
5 g protein
19 g carbohydrates

Variation:
- Substitute honey for the maple syrup, and vanilla extract for the maple extract.

Bran Muffins

Tangy dried currants and sweet grated apple blend with the spices in these muffins to produce moist, tender muffins that fill the kitchen with their aroma while baking.

Yield: 12 muffins | **Active time:** 10 minutes | **Start to finish:** 30 minutes

½ cup bran flake cereal
1½ cups whole-wheat flour
¾ teaspoon baking soda
¼ cup firmly packed dark brown sugar
½ teaspoon ground cinnamon
¼ teaspoon salt
¼ cup dried currants
⅓ cup orange juice
½ cup grated fresh apple
½ cup low-fat buttermilk
1 large egg, lightly beaten
1 tablespoon vegetable oil
Vegetable oil spray

1. Preheat the oven to 350°F, and grease muffin tins lightly with vegetable oil spray if not using a nonstick pan.
2. In one mixing bowl, combine cereal, whole-wheat flour, baking soda, brown sugar, cinnamon, and salt. Combine dried currants and orange juice in a small saucepan and bring to a boil over high heat. Pour mixture into another mixing bowl, and allow to cool for 5 minutes, then stir in apple, buttermilk, egg, and oil.
3. Stir liquids into dry ingredients, beating mixture with a wooden spoon to combine. Beat until combined but not overly smooth.
4. Divide batter evenly among the muffin tins, and bake in the center of the oven for 20–25 minutes, or until a toothpick inserted in the middle comes out clean. Place the pan on a rack to cool for 5 minutes, then remove muffins from the tins.

Note: The muffins can be prepared up to 1 day in advance and kept at room temperature, tightly covered. Reheat them, covered with aluminum foil, in a 300°F oven for 10–12 minutes for the best flavor.

Each reduced-calorie 1-muffin serving contains:
108 calories
18 calories from fat
2 g fat
0 g saturated fat
3 g protein
21 g carbohydrates

Variation:
- Substitute chopped dried apricots for the currants, and add 1 tablespoon chopped crystallized ginger to the batter.

There's a lot written today about "good carbs" and "bad carbs," and these muffins are an excellent example of "good carbs." There is no granulated sugar, nor is there any all-purpose flour; those are the foods to be avoided whenever possible.

Whole-Wheat Cranberry Muffins

Dried cranberries add a luscious red color as well as tangy, tart flavor to these easy-to-make muffins. These muffins are not very sweet, so they are as at home on the dinner table as the breakfast table.

Yield: 12 muffins | **Active time:** 10 minutes | **Start to finish:** 40 minutes

1½ cups whole-wheat flour
½ cup bran flake cereal
¼ cup granulated sugar
¾ teaspoon baking soda
½ teaspoon ground ginger
¼ teaspoon salt
1 cup low-fat buttermilk
1 tablespoon vegetable oil
1 large egg, lightly beaten
1 cup grated peeled apple
½ cup dried cranberries
Vegetable oil spray

1. Preheat the oven to 400°F, and grease muffin tins lightly with vegetable oil spray if not using a nonstick pan.
2. In one mixing bowl, combine flour, cereal, sugar, baking soda, ginger, and salt. In another mixing bowl, combine buttermilk, oil, egg, and apple.
3. Stir liquids into dry ingredients, beating mixture with a wooden spoon to combine. Beat until combined but not overly smooth. Stir in dried cranberries, mixing to distribute them evenly.
4. Divide batter evenly among the muffin tins, and bake in the center of the oven for 15–18 minutes, or until a toothpick inserted in the middle comes out clean. Place the pan on a rack to cool for 5 minutes, then remove muffins from the tins.

Note: The muffins can be prepared up to 1 day in advance and kept at room temperature, tightly covered. Reheat them, covered with aluminum foil, in a 300°F oven for 10–12 minutes for the best flavor.

Each reduced-calorie 1-muffin serving contains:

117 calories

19 calories from fat

2 g fat

0 g saturated fat

3.5 g protein

23 g carbohydrates

Variation:

- Substitute dried cherries or dried blueberries for the cranberries.

The grated apple in this recipe is what makes it possible to create muffins with only 1 tablespoon oil that have a pleasing mouth feel. The fruit supplies moisture, so you won't miss the fat.

Banana Bread

I adore banana bread, and this one delivers pure banana flavor—with very little fat—because it doesn't mask the fruit with cinnamon or other spices. This bread also freezes very well, so wrap the slices individually.

Yield: 12 slices | **Active time:** 15 minutes | **Start to finish:** 1¼ hours

½ cup firmly packed brown sugar
¼ cup granulated sugar
3 tablespoons unsalted butter, softened
1 large egg
3 large ripe bananas, peeled and mashed
2 tablespoons dark rum
½ teaspoon pure vanilla extract
2 cups all-purpose flour, plus extra for the loaf pan
1 teaspoon baking soda
1 teaspoon baking powder
¼ teaspoon salt

1. Preheat the oven to 350°F. Grease and flour a 9 x 5-inch loaf pan, knocking out any extra flour over the sink or a garbage can.
2. Combine brown sugar, granulated sugar, and butter in a mixing bowl and beat until light and fluffy. Stir in egg, bananas, rum, and vanilla, and beat until smooth. Sift flour, baking soda, baking powder, and salt together, and lightly beat into banana mixture.
3. Scrape batter into the prepared pan, smoothing the top. Bake in the center of the oven for 50–55 minutes, or until a toothpick inserted in the center comes out clean. Place the pan on a rack to cool for 5 minutes, then remove bread from the pan and cool it completely on a rack.

Note: The bread can be prepared up to 1 day in advance and kept at room temperature, tightly covered. Reheat individual slices, covered with aluminum foil, in a 300°F oven for 10–12 minutes for the best flavor.

Each reduced-calorie 1-slice serving contains:

143 calories

24 calories from fat

3 g fat

1.5 g saturated fat

2 g protein

27 g carbohydrates

Variation:

- Add ¾ cup chopped toasted nuts to the batter.

When bananas get too ripe to eat, don't throw them out and waste the money. Freeze them, right in the peel. When you're ready to make banana bread or a smoothie, just thaw the fruit in the microwave.

Carrot Bread

Carrot bread is a great way to sneak more vegetables into children's diets, as well as being a treat for adults, too. Like a traditional carrot cake, this bread is made with raisins and spices.

Yield: 12 slices | **Active time:** 15 minutes | **Start to finish:** 2 hours

1½ cups firmly packed finely grated carrot (about 4–5 carrots)

½ cup golden raisins

3 tablespoons unsalted butter

1½ cups water

¾ cup granulated sugar

1 large egg, lightly beaten

2 cups all-purpose flour, plus extra for the loaf pan

1 teaspoon baking soda

1 teaspoon baking powder

1 teaspoon ground cinnamon

¼ teaspoon salt

1. Combine carrot, raisins, butter, water, and sugar in a saucepan, and bring to a boil over medium heat. Simmer for 5 minutes, stirring frequently. Remove the pan from the heat, scrape mixture into a mixing bowl, and refrigerate until cooled, at least 45 minutes. Beat in egg, and set aside.

2. Preheat the oven to 350°F. Grease and flour a 9 x 5-inch loaf pan, knocking out any extra flour over the sink or a garbage can.

3. Sift flour, baking soda, baking powder, cinnamon, and salt together, and stir it into carrot mixture, beating with a wooden spoon.

4. Scrape batter into the prepared pan and bake in the center of the oven for 1 hour, or until a toothpick inserted in the center comes out clean. Place the pan on a rack to cool for 5 minutes, then remove bread from the pan and cool it completely on a rack.

Note: The bread can be prepared up to 1 day in advance and kept at room temperature, tightly covered. Reheat individual slices, covered with aluminum foil, in a 300°F oven for 10–12 minutes for the best flavor.

Each reduced-calorie 1-slice serving contains:

183 calories

32 calories from fat

4 g fat

2 g saturated fat

3 g protein

35.5 g carbohydrates

Variation:

- Add ¾ cup chopped toasted nuts to the batter.

Carrots are one of the world's wonder foods. Just one of these inexpensive root vegetables supplies more than twice your daily value of vitamin A, which is an essential nutrient to keep your immune system healthy.

Appendix A:
Metric Conversion Tables

The scientifically precise calculations needed for baking are not necessary when cooking conventionally. The tables in this appendix are designed for general cooking. If making conversions for baking, grab your calculator and compute the exact figure.

CONVERTING OUNCES TO GRAMS

The numbers in the following table are approximate. To reach the exact quantity of grams, multiply the number of ounces by 28.35.

Ounces	Grams
1 ounce	30 grams
2 ounces	60 grams
3 ounces	85 grams
4 ounces	115 grams
5 ounces	140 grams
6 ounces	180 grams
7 ounces	200 grams
8 ounces	225 grams
9 ounces	250 grams
10 ounces	285 grams
11 ounces	300 grams
12 ounces	340 grams
13 ounces	370 grams
14 ounces	400 grams
15 ounces	425 grams
16 ounces	450 grams

CONVERTING QUARTS TO LITERS

The numbers in the following table are approximate. To reach the exact amount of liters, multiply the number of quarts by 0.95.

Quarts	Liter
1 cup (1/4 quart)	1/4 liter
1 pint (1/2 quart)	1/2 liter
1 quart	1 liter
2 quarts	2 liters
2 1/2 quarts	2 1/2 liters
3 quarts	2 3/4 liters
4 quarts	3 3/4 liters
5 quarts	4 3/4 liters
6 quarts	5 1/2 liters
7 quarts	6 1/2 liters
8 quarts	7 1/2 liters

CONVERTING POUNDS TO GRAMS AND KILOGRAMS

The numbers in the following table are approximate. To reach the exact quantity of grams, multiply the number of pounds by 453.6.

Pounds	Grams; Kilograms
1 pound	450 grams
1 1/2 pounds	675 grams
2 pounds	900 grams
2 1/2 pounds	1,125 grams; 1 1/4 kilograms
3 pounds	1,350 grams
3 1/2 pounds	1,500 grams; 1 1/2 kilograms
4 pounds	1,800 grams
4 1/2 pounds	2 kilograms
5 pounds	2 1/4 kilograms
5 1/2 pounds	2 1/2 kilograms
6 pounds	2 3/4 kilograms
6 1/2 pounds	3 kilograms
7 pounds	3 1/4 kilograms
7 1/2 pounds	3 1/2 kilograms
8 pounds	3 3/4 kilograms

CONVERTING FAHRENHEIT TO CELSIUS

The numbers in the following table are approximate. To reach the exact temperature, subtract 32 from the Fahrenheit reading, multiply the number by 5, and then divide by 9.

Degrees Fahrenheit	Degrees Celsius
170°F	77°C
180°F	82°C
190°F	88°C
200°F	95°C
225°F	110°C
250°F	120°C
300°F	150°C
325°F	165°C
350°F	180°C
375°F	190°C
400°F	205°C
425°F	220°C
450°F	230°C
475°F	245°C
500°F	260°C

CONVERTING INCHES TO CENTIMETERS

The numbers in the following table are approximate. To reach the exact number of centimeters, multiply the number of inches by 2.54.

Inches	Centimeters
½ inch	1.5 centimeters
1 inch	2.5 centimeters
2 inches	5 centimeters
3 inches	8 centimeters
4 inches	10 centimeters
5 inches	13 centimeters
6 inches	15 centimeters
7 inches	18 centimeters
8 inches	20 centimeters
9 inches	23 centimeters
10 inches	25 centimeters
11 inches	28 centimeters
12 inches	30 centimeters

Appendix B:
Table of Weights and Measures of Common Ingredients

Food	Quantity	Yield
Apples	1 pound	2½–3 cups sliced
Avocado	1 pound	1 cup mashed
Bananas	1 medium	1 cup sliced
Bell peppers	1 pound	3–4 cups sliced
Blueberries	1 pound	3⅓ cups
Butter	¼ pound (1 stick)	8 tablespoons
Cabbage	1 pound	4 cups packed shredded
Carrots	1 pound	3 cups diced or sliced
Chocolate, morsels	12 ounces	2 cups
Chocolate, bulk	1 ounce	3 tablespoons grated
Cocoa powder	1 ounce	¼ cup
Coconut, flaked	7 ounces	2½ cups
Cream	½ pint (1 cup)	2 cups whipped
Cream cheese	8 ounces	1 cup
Flour	1 pound	4 cups
Lemons	1 medium	3 tablespoons juice
Lemons	1 medium	2 teaspoons zest
Milk	1 quart	4 cups
Molasses	12 ounces	1½ cups
Mushrooms	1 pound	5 cups sliced
Onions	1 medium	½ cup chopped
Peaches	1 pound	2 cups sliced
Peanuts	5 ounces	1 cup
Pecans	6 ounces	1½ cups
Pineapple	1 medium	3 cups diced
Potatoes	1 pound	3 cups sliced
Raisins	1 pound	3 cups
Rice	1 pound	2 to 2½ cups raw
Spinach	1 pound	¾ cup cooked
Squash, summer	1 pound	3½ cups sliced
Strawberries	1 pint	1½ cups sliced

Food	Quantity	Yield
Sugar, brown	1 pound	2¼ cups, packed
Sugar, confectioners'	1 pound	4 cups
Sugar, granulated	1 pound	2¼ cups
Tomatoes	1 pound	1½ cups pulp
Walnuts	4 ounces	1 cup

TABLE OF LIQUID MEASUREMENTS

Dash	=	less than $\frac{1}{8}$ teaspoon
3 teaspoons	=	1 tablespoon
2 tablespoons	=	1 ounce
8 tablespoons	=	½ cup
2 cups	=	1 pint
1 quart	=	2 pints
1 gallon	=	4 quarts

Index

Lemon Cheese Mousse, 230
Lemon Egg Soup, 50
little dishes. *See* appetizers; soups
Low-Cal Crispy Chicken, 74–75
low-calorie cooking techniques,
    17–20
Low-Cal Sloppy Joes, 138–39
Low-Cal Tuna Noodle Casserole,
    186–87
loyalty cards, 6

Macaroni with White Beans,
    Tomatoes, and Sage, 218
Manhattan Clam Chowder, 150–51
Maple Bourbon Frozen
    Yogurt, 237
marinating, 15, 26, 183
measures, table of, 249–50
meat, processed, 17
metric conversion tables, 246–48
Mexican Fish with Olives, 164–65
Mexican Spaghetti Squash, 214–15
Mexican Tomato Sauce, 39
Mocha Mousse, 231
mousses
    Lemon Cheese Mousse, 230
    Mocha Mousse, 231
    modifying recipes for, 13
Mushrooms Stuffed with Spinach
    and Feta, 64–65

nuts, 16

oil, in stir-frying, 19
online shopping, 10–11
Oven-Fried Chicken Fingers with
    Sweet Potato Fries, 72–73
overbuying, 8

Pasta Primavera, 216–17
Pear Clafoutis, 233
Pear Dressing, 25
Phyllo Egg Rolls, 66–67
planning, weekly, 1–3
pork
    about, 110–12
    Grilled Pork Ensalata, 112–13
    Japanese Pork Balls on Wilted
        Spinach, 126–27

Key West Pork Salad with
    Oranges, 120–21
Lasagna Rolls, 128–29
Pork Chops with Chutney, 122–23
Pork Ragu, 124–25
Spicy Pork in Garlic Sauce, 116–17
Stir-Fried Pork Lo Mein, 114–15
stock for, 125
Stuffed Peppers with Sausage
    and Egg, 130–31
Traditional New Mexican Pozole,
    118–19
Pork Chops with Chutney, 122–23
Pork Ragu, 124–25
portion sizes, 15, 17
potatoes
    Broccoli-Stuffed Baked Potatoes,
        208–9
    Fish with Onions and Potatoes,
        166–67
    Oven-Fried Chicken Fingers with
        Sweet Potato Fries, 72–73
price per unit, 6–7
processed foods, 16–17

rebates, 5
Rhode Island Clam Chowder,
    148–49
Rice Pudding, 228–29
roll cutting, 18
Rosemary Vinaigrette, 27

salad bars, supermarket, 9
salad dressings. *See* dressings
salads
    Asian Steak Salad, 134–35
    Free-Style Tuna Salad
        Niçoise, 185
    Key West Pork Salad with
        Oranges, 120–21
    Spanish Chicken Salad, 94–95
    Spicy Beef, Pasta, and Mushroom
        Salad, 136–37
    as starter, 21
    Tuna and Garbanzo Bean
        Salad, 188
sauces
    Asian Mussels in Black Bean
        Sauce, 152–53